THE SECRETS OF SUCCESSFUL WOMEN 2024 EDITION

By Sharon Brown

The Book Chief

25th April 2024

Thank you so much for your support tonight :)

with love Naomi Richs x

Published by The Book Chief Publishing House 2024
Suite 2A, Blackthorn House, St Paul's Square, Birmingham, B3 1RL
www.thebookchief.com

Book Cover Design: Deearo Marketing
Editor: Sharon Brown
Typesetting: Sharon Brown
Publishing: Sharon Brown

THE BOOK CHIEF®
IGNITE YOUR WRITING

Table of Contents

Introduction

In the pages of "The Secrets of Successful Women", we embark on an illuminating journey into the lives of remarkable women who have shattered ceilings, defied norms, and carved their paths to success in all areas of lives.

In this, the second of our Successful Women projects, we uncover more areas of success through the lens of these extraordinary women. Their tales serve as both inspiration and a roadmap, offering invaluable insights into the multifaceted nature of achievement. Whether it's conquering corporate ladders, nurturing families, pioneering in science and technology, or leading social change movements, the stories within these highlight the ways women are leaving their powerful mark on history, community and society.

Each chapter unveils the strategies, sacrifices, and resilience that underpin their success.

Beyond the individual stories, this book delves into universal themes of ambition, resilience, empowerment, and the pursuit of purpose. It challenges conventional notions of success, inviting readers to explore its nuances across different cultures, generations, and circumstances.

"The Secrets of Successful Women" is not only a celebration of achievement but a testament to the transformative power of ambition, perseverance, and solidarity. As we delve into the triumphs and tribulations of these extraordinary women, may their stories inspire, empower, and guide us on our own journeys toward success, whatever form it may take.

Foreword

By Naomi Riches MBE PLY DL

It is a rare thing to find a group of women who are ready to be so open and who are willing to be so brave in sharing their secrets to success in such a public way. In these pages, you will read stories that are honest, that are raw, and that are relatable; the special quality throughout is that each author has remained true to themselves. These shared secrets may bring tears to your eyes or send shivers down your spine… but you will also read about moments that warm your heart and make you think!

When I was asked to be part of this book, I simply could not say no. What an opportunity to share something so important to me, something that has been a vital part of my personal story and the backbone of my success. I feel extremely privileged to be part of this book and to be published alongside these incredible women.

I know the other women in these stories feel the same way and many have jumped at the opportunity to be published with each other and in this publication.

This opportunity would not be possible for any of us without the guiding hand of Sharon Brown, our Lead Creator of this book and Founder of The Book Chief Publishing House.

Sharon is passionate about creating real opportunities for small business owners to build credibility and visibility through writing, speaking and publishing. The first book in the series, The Secrets of 99 Successful Women, was published in 2023 and was such a great success that Sharon didn't think twice about continuing the series… so here we are, The Secrets of Successful Women Volume Two.

The Book Chief is a multi-award winning Indie Publishing House and is driven by its want to give its Authors maximum exposure. Born during the pandemic, they have published over 250 Authors from over 15 countries around the world.

Being part of this has not only helped me to understand more about myself, delving into memories I had not explored for a while… but it has also opened my eyes to the variety of amazing stories that are out there, just waiting to be told.

I have been inspired and uplifted… I hope you are too.

Dedication

To every little girl who feels she is not worthy

To every little girl who feels she won't have the opportunities to rise

To every little girl who feels she doesn't fit in

To every little girl who tries to dim her light to suit others

To every little girl.....YOU CAN AND YOU WILL FEEL SUCCESS

MRES FRECKLES
2024

CHAPTER 1

Silenced not silent. Desperate to determined

By Mrs Freckles

Success

What is success to me and do I consider myself successful? In short, yes and no! Let me explain what I mean.

You can be successful in many ways, from a high-flying career to winning the lottery or finding the right person to spend your life with. Is that all that can be measured as successful? What do you think? It's very subjective and individual. What may be success for one may not be for another.

For me, my measure of success is different. It's more than the tangible or material things. It's more than what can be achieved in a career or educational accomplishments. It's the process of time that has been spent dealing with historical past events, especially when those events link to trauma. In brief, historically, I have lived through extreme trauma that spanned years, involving numerous people. This chapter is not to portray or highlight any of the trauma I have endured, merely to share the insights I have gained along the way, and the highs and lows of the journey itself. I want to give hope to anyone who has ever felt any of the dark, deep-rooted, and twisted things that I have felt. A hope that things can, in time, get better. A hope that this is not all there is. A hope that allows you to see you are so much more than your trauma-soaked past.

I've learned along the way that there are so many ways of coping with such experiences. There are all too familiar stories of those who turn to drugs, alcohol, or both. Some live reckless lifestyles, and some withdraw within themselves, trying desperately to hide and pretend 'it' didn't even happen. Who am I to judge the journey of others? In some form or another, we all have difficult things to deal with, and we are all just trying to cope by whatever means. Who's to say what's the right or the wrong way? Who decides what works or what doesn't? Are we all the same? We all deal with things differently, to the best of our ability, and that is OK. In some way, we are all just trying to make it through the day.

History

When I first started on this journey, as it's been called, many who felt they 'knew best' claimed that I needed to have therapy. And so, I did. I took the path of finding a therapist to support me through what was happening in my head, my body, and every part of my being. At the time, I was 15/16, with no income and no clue where to begin. I was a timid, vulnerable teen living in unsavoury conditions. Somehow, during the conflict, I found a specialist service that offered counselling. At first, this seemed like the best option; it focused on the exact thing I had experienced. Sessions were heavy and hard, detailing the traumatic event that led me through their door. While I was open to talking to them, I still didn't know or understand why I was there or what good it would do. Nobody thought to explain how being there could help me. Nor was I able to ask that very question. At this stage, I hadn't even accepted what had happened to me, let alone get help and support with it. There was very little support for a woman like me, with the type of specialist services that could handle my history.

I tried different avenues, from begging for help via my GP practice, to seeing numerous private therapists and some charities that offered free sessions. Every time, I thought it 'would work' for me. I thought I could work through my pain, my distress, of all that had happened. Doctors were less than helpful, and I didn't belong under the mental health team when what I was going through was emotional more than it was mental health related. Doctors medicated me and tried to just deal with the symptoms rather than the root cause of my distress. My concerns were met with a solution focused on masking the issue rather than facing it head-on with the proper support. There were often blanket options that everyone would be given, rather than individual options to my needs.

Nothing was easy or straightforward, and it often felt like a fight, a battle I desperately tried to win. But what was winning? I always felt I didn't fit the mould of the service I had approached. My issues were severe; I needed one-to-one support with the right type of therapist. I didn't belong in many of the counselling services that could offer me sessions. My lack of trust in anyone also proved to be a hindrance to therapy. I had reason not to trust. I had been let down repeatedly by all the organisations that could help remove me from the dire situation I was in; teachers, social services, the police, etc. They were not interested in anything I had to say and I quite often felt dismissed. Can you imagine, as a young, vulnerable adult, how it felt to have tried to get help and then for it to be effectively slammed in your face? Can you imagine the pain of that? Can you imagine the stress and how much energy it took to even say any of those things to adults that were seemingly supposed to help?

Over the years, more investment into support services and charities that could handle these things finally afforded me the opportunity to talk. During especially distressing times, endless conversations with helpline support workers were had, detailing and discussing things that didn't feel quite right. It was during this time that I was able to fully learn the true extent of what I had endured, where I was able to really explore and acknowledge these harrowing experiences. The magnitude and severity of these traumatic events really hammered home during those conversations. While the purpose of this is not to detail each experience, it feels important to highlight the impact and consequences of their very real and raw nature. It also feels important to try to, in some small way, emphasise the lengths I went to for help, but I was often met with adverse responses if any at all.

It took a long time to find the right therapist, years and years, to help work through all that happened. Often, the first person or the first avenue isn't right. Several times, I thought I had found a 'good one' only to later discover I had hastily misplaced the little trust I had started to form. This took its toll, in the form of starting over becoming increasingly more difficult. Trying to be open when facing those who were not interested was tough. But I persisted; I was stubborn (well, I'm still stubborn!), and I was not going to be quiet anymore. This fight in my belly took many forms. What's been described as determination throughout it all has kept me from totally breaking down. I have had to face crippling episodes of depression and anxiety as a result of CPTSD across those years.

I'd been dismissed by therapists previously, or they were less understanding in nature. I found some that could not grasp what I was trying to share. It was not at all easy and certainly not plain sailing. My current therapist has been working with me for a little over two years. I'm now in a place I have never been before. While I wouldn't say that my 'journey' to healing and self-actualisation is complete, I am remarkedly further ahead than I have ever been. We've had endless hours of discussing the same thing sometimes, but from a different perspective, to process their impact on my life now whilst trying to release those emotions that have built up.

So, how did I get there? Simply – with intense work! Trust was necessary; I couldn't just work with 'anyone'. They had to be compassionate, open to hearing every minute detail, and challenge me where appropriate. I needed someone calm enough to handle my eccentricities, manage the tangents I may run with, or simply sit with me in silence. They had to be willing to work with me long-term to allow me the time to process these events. I had to pace myself so that I wasn't in the depths of dissociation and to still be a functioning adult in the world. Throughout it all, I have encountered trials and tribulations. My current therapist's acknowledgement, validation, and reassurance has humbled me. I discovered my own voice. The one I wasn't ever allowed to use before. I stopped blaming myself – but this took YEARS! Different approaches work well for me. I'm logical but also creative. I use writing as a way of expressing myself and to figuratively 'send letters' to those involved in my past. I quite often use music as my go-to. I 'feel' the lyrics, the pounding baseline, or the insane vocal talents of artists. I find meaning in those words, those that mimic my own feelings.

Self-expression

Some of the techniques we have attempted have been challenging. I'd like to briefly touch on a few, as they were significant. 'One 'trial' I was asked to look in the mirror.' Sounds simple, right? The essence is very simple: just looking in the mirror. The purpose was to look into my own eyes and notice things about myself/my face that I hadn't before. It was an attempt to lessen the conflict I held about myself. It's one I'm continuing to embrace. Another such technique relates to the 'Bill of Rights' in the USA. For this, I had to come up with (as best I could) ten 'rights' that I have. I surprisingly managed to write <u>50</u>! Below are just a few I'd like to highlight.

I have a right to…

- Breathe.
- Speak/talk about the things that have happened.

- Love and be loved.
- Be me/who I am/embrace the 'gayness'.
- Learn – about anything/everything.
- Feel – be angry or sad at the things I endured.
- Medicine – medical treatments and attention.
- Express myself.
- Therapy and healing.

These are just a few from that list. Ultimately, I discovered that many things were a right to just be me, just to live freely. It emphasised how the essentials of life were missing. Try your own; what do you have a right to? Take some time to think about that. Discovering what may be missing or needed to enrich your life is significant.

Another technique I adopted years back is my love of writing. Taking inspiration from my pain, I journaled and wrote poems. I'd like to share one of my poems here. It details many deep-rooted feelings I was unsure how to handle or where to place them. It's raw, it's real, and it's an ongoing process.

Nothingness

For all this torment I'm going through, here in my heart because of you.

Of all the things you were meant to be, except you couldn't be that for me.

The mother I needed, one just to care, to show affection and simply be there.

But you left, without a second thought, with no regard to my feeling distraught.

The ache so deep, dark, and twisted inside, a maternal figure, always was I denied.

Just a fraught little girl, unloved, all alone, living in a toxic, scary, broken home.

Do you smile knowing you did all this? Did you even realise how much you would miss?

Of me, your daughter, the one you left behind, was it out of sight, then out of your mind?

What was so great about drinking like that? Tossed aside, just so matter of fact.

Nothingness is all that's left inside my heart, the one that you broke; it's left torn apart.

You did this, not me; I'm left so numb, holding onto that, trying not to succumb.

Or take all the blame and responsibility, it was you, mother, you abandoned me.

Just a fragile child, a little girl just six, Caught in the baggage, up in all the mix.

Of destruction that followed in your stink, given in to the booze and all that you'd drink.

All day, all night, in fact, every single day, nothing excuses you for behaving this way.

It's that time of year again, the day you died, all this pain sitting so heavy, yet to subside.

Will I ever be able to get past that missing part, the mother I crave, this ache in my heart.

Forever felt, for all my life, will it ever go away? Or will it just haunt me now and every day?

Just face facts, motherless and empty I'll be, continuing to crave that love maternally.

Lost, on my own again, as it's been til now, no one to depend, fighting through somehow.

And so, it continues, a life that feels undone, the end, I lost, that means you won.

I've faced the all singing and dancing critical self-voice. Battling my own internal demons. Facing, often head-on, beliefs from my formative years that led me to feel unworthy, weak, and powerless. Am I those things? No! No! While I still battle these thoughts and feelings, for the most part, the progression I have made has been to break down those walls, those barriers of my own internal struggle. It comes from the voice that learned negative talk. I am beginning to learn that I am more than my history. I am learning that I am worthy of more than I could ever believe. I'm discovering beauty in the little and big things and embracing it as best I can. The work I am now able to do in therapy is profound. It is far-reaching and deeper than it could ever have been before. It's taken so much patience on both my part and that of my therapist.

The point of writing this way is to show how far I have come from when I blamed myself for everything. I was being swallowed up in depression and constant angst and not at all in a place to heal. Despite my trying, despite my continual efforts to see counsellors/therapists, I remained in the same 'stuck' place for years. Until I understood why I was there. What was the point? The result of this hard work is to feel healed, whole even. As I continue, the point is to dedicate space for this work with time never afforded before. A safe space to explore the depths of these experiences. Outside of trauma, a place to learn who I am, perhaps for the first time.

Without trying to sound condescending or hypocritical, no one-size-fits-all. It's a matter of discovering what works for you and what helps you. Do you gel with them? Can they truly hear what you have to say? Talking therapy may not be the answer for everyone. There are many different forms of support, and finding what works for you is vital. You are the expert in you. It takes patience, courage, and strength to face such atrocities. All things you may feel don't exist within yourself. I've felt those things over and over and in different forms. But I am doing it, the work to reach a place of healing, of leaving the past where it belongs. It is a long process, but you are worth it – and so am I.

Tips and tricks that helped

When dealing with such difficult situations and all that comes up when processing trauma, there have been some tricks I have found along the way. Grounding – learning to breathe (odd, I know when we do this without thinking!), but it's the kind of focused breathing technique I'm referring to here. There are many ways of being more grounded/in the 'here and now' (a phrase that used to make me shudder!). From counting in for 4, holding, and breathing out for 6, to long, slow breaths. Allowing each breath to reach the pit of your tummy. There's one which I found somewhat helpful called the 54321. There are many variants of this one. In its simplest form, it's about naming five things you can see, four things you can touch, three things you can hear, two things you can smell, and a final deep breath at the end. An alternative may be to name five things you can see in blue and four red things, etc. It may be obvious, but the idea is to get the mind to re-focus on where it's at now – the present. A toolkit of these techniques can help, like having a physical box with things that are soft to the touch or a nice fragrance, etc.

What's next for me?

Reading this through, I can see what I have achieved more clearly. As I continue this journey, I hope to find that release of emotion and genuinely believe who I am becoming is good enough. I plan to continue writing and expressing myself in any way I can. One day, I may even have a book of my very own. I want to find a way to be a pivotal influence in someone else's fight for recovery and healing.

Thank you for taking the time to follow the path I briefly shared. I hope it can give hope to those struggling. It may not be ok now, but it will be with patience and hard work. Don't ever give up on yourself!

“

Every woman's success should be an inspiration to another. We're STRONGEST when we cheer each other on.

SERENA WILLIAMS

GILLIAN ROUTLEDGE

2024

CHAPTER 2

Secrets of my Soul

By Gillian Routledge

What do I mean by 'Secrets of my Soul'? I believe that the real essence of a fulfilled life lies in living with purpose. It's about understanding how life nudges us towards our purpose, often in mysterious ways we can't initially comprehend.

As I become increasingly connected to my soul's yearning to write, I'm grateful for recently achieving the milestone of being a published author. Sharing my book, 'Discovering the Love Within,' which already has glowing reviews, feels almost surreal. It wasn't always this way. I'm eager to share insights on tapping into the depths of your soul and overcoming the hurdles hindering our ability to write and share our stories. Before delving into that, I'd like to share a childhood memory that significantly shaped my journey. It's a tale of overcoming adversity and rediscovering my love for writing.

It's 1969; for that ten-year-old me, it's another ordinary day, and yet this day impacts the course of my life and my dreams. I'm sitting behind a well-worn desk, staring at the ink well, which has blackened over the years, and my fingers are tracing the indents of carved initials in the wood. The old church school windows across the room shed a little light on this gloomy classroom. He is standing there, his body is ruler straight in front of his desk.

His thick-rimmed glasses add to the image of severity. The familiar moss-green exercise book is held between his bony fingers, curled at the edges. I hear his commanding voice silence the room. "*Today, I have chosen to read Gillian's beautiful story."* I can feel my face flushing hot and bright red. My head is bowed low, feeling vulnerable and wishing I could disappear into the wall behind me.

How would you have felt in this situation? Maybe you are proud or excited about having your work acknowledged.

Not me because I felt that writing was a private and personal thing that was not for sharing with anyone, and it never crossed my mind that my deepest feelings would be exposed in this way. I felt that being pretty much mediocre with unexceptional results gave me the luxury of being invisible. Not now. The spotlight was on this freak of a girl who wrote openly and maybe too honestly about her feelings. The feeling in this moment was pure fear as the head teacher continued to read, an instinctual urge to run and flee from a classroom of junior critics who could be cruel and heartless at the best of times. Instead, my fingers were gripped together underneath the desk, knuckles tight and white, praying for this embarrassing moment to end. This is just the beginning, and break time would allow the young gangsters to have free reign to taunt and ridicule me. In that silent prayer to myself, the words were: *"I will never put myself in this position again."* Something inside shuts down, and that creative gift of writing went under lock and key. What that child didn't realise was that a part of me died that day.

The discovery since has been that the promises we make in our younger years can continue to impact us on a subconscious level. That is until a wake-up call comes along.

Moving forward thirty-plus years. It's 3 am, and words in poetic form are flooding through me like an electric current, waking me from a deep sleep; there is no rest or choice until I fumble in the dark for pen and paper, taking myself into the hotel bathroom for privacy to scrawl the first poem written since that younger me made a promise to cut ties to this gift.

The poetry awoke something in me that now cannot sleep again. At that time, I was training in a powerful healing modality that I now know opened up my innate creative gift of poetry and writing.

We all carry a unique story woven from our experiences, dreams and emotions. This tale shapes our identity and influences how we perceive and interact with the world around us.

As I delved deeper into uncovering the mysteries that stirred me from a slumber of indifference, I realised the profound impact that childhood memories wield over our adult lives. Those early experiences, seemingly innocuous at the time, cast long shadows on our relationships, work and our very essence. They shape our beliefs and habits and often contribute to feeling trapped, unfulfilled, or as if part of us has withered away.

I remember vividly feeling like I was living someone else's life, a puppet dancing to the tunes and expectations that were not my own. It was as if I operated on automatic pilot until a breaking point forced me to kneel deep in prayer as if pleading for help. Surrendering in that moment sparked a profound shift within me.

Have you ever reached a point where seeking help seemed to open a new door, where vulnerability led to newfound strength?

I've come to cherish life's experiences that guided me back to my innate passion for writing, a connection to my inner child. I discovered that breaking through the barriers we build around our creativity is complex. For me, it took years of unlocking old beliefs about achieving what was possible. It became a process of identifying old vows I had made to myself that were sabotaging me in the guise of keeping me safe. Little by little, I learned to tap into resources I never knew I possessed, such as becoming more self-confident, believing in myself, and loving parts of me I thought were unlovable. Now, I can look in the mirror and genuinely love what I see regardless of visible signs of ageing.

Maintaining a journalling practice consistently and regularly has helped with releasing and letting go of the old judgements. A critical mindset kept me stuck in the conditioned, destructive, self-sabotaging patterns that held me firmly in my comfort zone. This place held me in the known. I now believe growth can only occur when we step into unknown territory and make different choices. The wake-up call starts when the place of comfort becomes too uncomfortable to remain in the loop of the same old cycles of behaviour. This is the point when we are more willing to implement change, then learning and growth can take place incrementally and naturally. It feels as if an inner guidance pulls us in a direction only our soul is aware of.

What I mean by learning and growth is more of an unlearning, letting go of conditioned habits or programming from parents or society along with beliefs we hold to be true.

For instance, I once believed I could never achieve my dream of becoming a writer because I didn't consider myself intelligent enough. I constantly compared myself to what I perceived as intellectual intelligence, giving it more value while undermining or completely overlooking the presence of a profound emotional intelligence – a gift I now recognise as significant. Allow me to highlight some practical steps that I believe are fundamental to achieving success as a writer.

Before I delve into the practical steps, I've learnt from personal experience that unravelling the layers of old promises we make to protect ourselves is crucial. Therapy and support played pivotal roles in releasing the emotional scars that held me back. Only then did adopting a consistent writing practice come into play.

It's not about producing a masterpiece; sometimes, it's about allowing the words to flow without censorship or expecting anything in return. Allowing words to spill out onto a page creates space for something more profound to arise. I've condensed the journey into an acronym. **'WRITE'** to simplify the steps.

W - willingness to allow writing to happen naturally, without overthinking.

R – reflect on pivotal moments from your past and reignite that inner spark

I - initiate the internal emotional response to rediscovering your gift

T – time dedicated regularly and consistently to putting words on paper

E - evoke emotions that connect and create a commonality with your reader.

These steps might seem simple, but they hold immense power. They are the breadcrumbs to the authentic, creative self we once shut down.

Let's break down these simple yet powerful steps one by one.

Starting with 'W' for willingness – it might sound easy to allow writing to flow naturally, but it's often far from it. Overcoming the resistance built over the years, designed to shield us from vulnerability, can take time. It's not just about letting go of overthinking; it's about embracing mindfulness, which requires patience and persistent observation of our thoughts without attachment to them. It's a subject that warrants its own deep dive.

Moving on to 'R' for reflection – delving into our past, especially our childhood, unveils forgotten aspirations. Do you remember those dreams, the ambitions that faded as we grew into responsible adults? Writing has an incredible ability to reignite that fading flame, feeding that fire within.

'I' signifies initiating an emotional response to rediscover your gift. Invite your emotions to be expressed and make friends with them instead of treating them as your enemy. Think of a powerful film that stirs a multitude of emotions within you. That emotional connection is akin to what writing can evoke, tapping into a myriad of feelings from sorrow to joy, rekindling our passion. Like many, I, for one, love a good weepy love story.

Then 'T' for time. Allocating this precious commodity to ourselves can be a rocky path strewn with distractions and obstacles. Often, it is easier to devote time to others, leaving our own needs unmet. This can often lead to feelings of frustration and even resentment. Yet, when we prioritise our well-being without expecting others to fulfil our needs, a shift occurs. We become happier, more creative and better company to hang out with.

Lastly, 'E' urges us to evoke emotions that connect us with our readers, even if that reader is just ourselves. It is crucial to recognise the value of connecting with these emotions rather than burying them. Suppressing our emotions isn't just detrimental to our mental health; it impacts us on a physical and soul level as well.

It's not just about believing in the soul; it's about honouring that part of ourselves, acknowledging and accepting that aspect. Because when we ignore our soul's purpose, it can make life feel colourless, like walking through a mist, disconnected.

It took me years to navigate through that fog, learning that adversity can be a catalyst for growth. Embracing gratitude shifted my perspective and allowed me to let go of the victimhood. Acceptance of each moment and embracing the journey were the keys to a revitalised way of living. This has been a journey often taken walking side by side with others on a similar path where we have held and supported each other along the way, with moments of crying and laughing together. Sometimes, it has taken courage and humility to ask for help from those with experience to guide me along the way. To trust that inner knowing, when to listen to others and when to listen to the truth of our gut instinct. To say thank you for well-intentioned advice, take on board what feels right. The key, however, is to follow your heart and soul because we all have access to the greatness of who we are.

So, have you ever felt that internal call toward something greater? That gentle tug urging you to explore and share your story? Trust me, despite the fear, embracing this journey is profoundly rewarding. It's a journey worth taking.

"

I am thankful for my struggle because, without it, I wouldn't have stumbled across my strength.

ALEX ELLE

HEATHER WILDMAN
2024

CHAPTER 3

A Blessing in Disguise

By Heather Wildman

I was feeling lost and frustrated. It was 2012 and at 41 years of age, I knew I needed to do something, or I would lose myself, or go mad.

I have always lived and been involved in agriculture. As a child, I was lucky to be raised on a farm where we could make camps in the hay barn, help lamb the sheep, and feed and play with the orphan lambs and calves. It was pretty idyllic, and I have never lost my love for farming and the countryside.

I had heard of several people in my network who had applied for a Nuffield Farming Scholarship and seen the huge difference it had made to them and for them. It felt right, but it also felt a huge challenge. I applied to study "Communication - how to influence and motivate change". This is a scholarship that you need to apply for. You just submit a topic you want to study that would help UK farming, agriculture, and industry in the future. If your application was approved, you had a thorough in-person interview with approximately 12 people for 20 minutes, which in reality felt more like an interrogation! Those lucky enough to be awarded their scholarship then receive a bursary of approx. £7,000 to help fund their travel, for which you are expected to be away from home and family and work for at least eight weeks. On your return, you write a paper and present it at the national conference in front of around 400 people. I had never done anything like this before, so it was a leap of faith!

I had left school at 15 with basic GCSE's and I never went to college or university. I joined the NatWest bank, but I hated this and soon left and moved into the other side of sales. I was naturally good at this; I liked people, and I liked to talk. My career moved and progressed and I got married and moved from Cumbria to Scotland for my husband's work. I had two gorgeous daughters, but I felt trapped. Was it a mid-life crisis?

I routinely felt misunderstood or a square peg in a round whole. I had some fantastic jobs working in agriculture for people and companies whom I admired, but routinely, once a new manager came in, things would break down, politics and beaurocracy would become stifling and resulted in me being told to conform, not to be so outspoken, to tone it down. "Heather, do not challenge".

Nuffield came through and blew me away; it was a hard place to win your seat, and the expectations of you are high, but so were the opportunities. Here, you were actively encouraged to challenge everything, to continuously ask questions, and to always question the why. It was 11 weeks of selfish travel, adventure, and learning. I visited Chile, Peru, Brazil, Australia, New Zealand, Canada & America, Ireland & Wales. It was the most amazing adventure. I was sailing up the Amazon, locked in a high-security prison in Penetanguishene, Canada, cowboying in Montana (Yellowstone eat your heart out!). I met with incredible businesses, people, companies and families from government, IT, psychology, knowledge transfer, research, farming, ranches, entrepreneurs, coaching and mentoring. It was such a privilege; people let you into their businesses, families, and lives. They were incredibly open and honest, sharing their highs and successes and trusting you with their lows, greatest failings and hardest lessons. It was an extremely humbling and moving experience.

When I had completed my travels and returned in 2014, I wrote my paper. I had come up with a genius idea about what my new career, my driver, and my future would be. I was completely bought into the belief that The Scottish Dairy Hub would be a one-stop shop where anyone involved at whatever level or context in the Scottish dairy industry could go to find out what was happening, information, contacts, learning, etc. It would be a game changer, and I was the person to do this.

I was sold on my concept. I put a proposal and tender together to the Scottish government. They loved the idea -"Yes, Heather, we will back this with 50% funding for 3 years. You just need to get the remaining 50% funding". After many conversations with organisations and industry, my existing employer said they also believed in the value, idea and concept and would match the remaining 50% of funding. This was not the route I had hoped for so I was nervous about this as

I wanted complete independence, but you have to start somewhere. They assured me that it was not easy to start a new business and how complicated it could be, so I went with it (how naïve was I?) but, Ding Dong, we are off and on our way! But then my fears became a reality; I was told that as it was being funded by public money, everything had to go through a tender. The position had to be advertised nationally. I had to apply .... I was starting to get a bad feeling, but whenever I aired this, I was always reassured: "Who else could run this and make it a success? It was my baby?"

How wrong I was; I will never forget sitting in front of the interview panel. I felt the interview went well; I came out into the car park thinking, "Yes, you smashed that girl", when I met another gentleman in the car park heading into the interview room…....mmm actually, he could do this job...mmm. I was put out of my misery two days later when I received the call to say thank you for applying, but unfortunately, I was not successful.

I was crushed, I was devastated, I could not believe it. I had put everything into this and told the world how great this would be. Look out and watch Heather influence and transform the Scottish dairy industry… I was a girl who thought big!! I was humiliated, embarrassed and also ashamed. What now? What would people think?

I wrote a social media post pulling on my big girl pants. I posted that I would like to congratulate the new manager on his new post, wish him and the organisation all the best, and ask everyone to get behind them. Then I handed in my notice to my employer as I felt betrayed and out manoeuvred and cried and cried and cried. I slipped into a dark, depressed and shattered place. I was lost, and I was very, very low. This shocked my family and also highlighted who my friends were. Those who I had thought would be there for me but stayed away, did not return my calls, and did not want to be associated with my failure!

My family had never seen me like this. I was always the strong, upbeat, bubbly person. "Come on, pull yourself together, give yourself a shake; tomorrow is another day!"

But not this time; this time, I just wanted to crawl into a hole and die.

This continued, and some weeks later, an old industry colleague contacted me. "Heather, a few of us have been talking, and we are worried about you. “I want you to think about five things you will achieve in 5 years, and I will call you back in 2 weeks." Hmph... I initially felt sorry for myself and continued to sulk and mope, "I'm not good enough to do anything…:" but I eventually got to thinking, and I came up with my five year plan.

1. To be seen and respected as a specialist in my field
2. To influence & motivate positive change in a job that fulfils me
3. Work-life balance that encompasses friends & family
4. Own a second home
5. Own a motorhome

That phone call in March 2014 resulted in me starting my own company Saviour Associates Ltd (Saviour Ass– saving asses and kicking asses), influencing and motivating positive change, soft skills with a sledgehammer in June 2014. (It turns out it is relatively easy to start a new company!).

I focused on what I had learnt on my Nuffield travels and built a business with a simple concept.

Regardless of who I am working for, the sector or industry, the scale and size, I always start with the following:

Vision – where are you, where do you want to be, and how will you get there?

Communication – who do you need to share your vision with, what do they need to know, in what format, and how often do we need to communicate?

Collaboration – do you have the skills to achieve your vision? If not, how do you get these, and do you have the right people alongside you fulfilling the right roles?

Initially, I focused on the UK dairy market and industry, assisting with staff management, recruitment, motivation, and team building. I knew this industry and sector well, and I was well-known and respected. I also set up and facilitated dairy business discussion groups.

In 2015, I developed and initiated a new leadership programme for the Scottish Association of Young Farmers Club, the Cultivating Leaders, a 6-day course split over four months with 3 x 2-day sessions.

Day 1: Who are you, where are you, what do you want to be and do, and what is leadership, personality profiling, and goal setting?

Day 2: Delivered by land agents who shared routes into agriculture, the future of UK agriculture, potential contracts, and opportunities with us. We also have a lawyer to discuss business structures, partnership agreements, and how to approach succession.

One-Month later

Day 3: Delivered by an Accountant on how to use your accounts and your accountant, online accounting, and the importance of having the right business ownership and structure.

Day 4: Bank representatives talking about debt, borrowing money, getting the best from your bank manager and completing a successful business plan.

Two-Months later

Day 5: Visiting other farming businesses, new entrants, diversification and family businesses. These owners share their stories and lessons and offer life tips and advice to the group.

Day 6: Visit to the Scottish Government at Holyrood in Edinburgh. Meeting MPs who shared with us how we can get involved in government and help ensure our government leaders have the best advice possible.

The course closes with each participant giving a personal 7-minute presentation to their family, press, sponsors, and industry leaders.

This course is a mini Scottish Enterprise Rural Leadership and Nuffield Farming Scholarship. It aims to stretch people and grow them when they are younger (rather than waiting until they are 40!) and to recognise the value and importance of investing in yourself and taking time away from home, work and family. It's written with my personal message of what I wish someone had said to me when I was in my early 20s, and it is one of the greatest things I have been involved in; I am incredibly proud to see these young farmers grow and develop through the programme and then to watch and see their careers grow as the years move on. We are delivering our 8th year in Scotland and piloting the same course in Northern Ireland.

So, looking back to that terrible time in 2014 when I thought my career and life was over, what have I achieved since then?

- I now own three houses
- I purchased my motorhome in 2018 (The Fun Bus). I regularly use this as my mode of transport and accommodation as I travel all over the UK. We have just enjoyed 3.5 weeks of touring through France, Italy and Switzerland.
- My business has grown and flourished. I am recognised as a specialist in my field and a keynote speaker in family succession, staff management and motivation, leadership and resilience. I have a name and brand that is recognised UK-wide and globally.
- I do make a positive difference, and I have been told that I help change people's lives.
- I have wonderful friends and family who I never take for granted.
- I have the best job in the world!

Now, my challenging and questioning personality is seen as a strength and a skill that people and companies value. They want straight talking.

I have clients in all walks of life and industry from NHS, Accountants, land agents, government, farmers, vineyards, estates, and even His Majesty the King is a client too...not bad, eh, for a wee lass from Cumbria who left school at 15!

I now get paid to travel and talk all over the UK and overseas. Thank goodness I did not get that job. Thank goodness I grabbed that opportunity to apply for a Nuffield Farming Scholarship; thank goodness that person picked up the phone and challenged me.

Tough times don't last; tough people do, and as my granny always said, "Heather, what is meant for you won't go by you."

So think big, think bold, and every day, do one thing to get you closer to that dream and goal. Do not fear failure; make sure you learn from it and bounce forward.

JO HOWARTH

2024

CHAPTER 4

True Success

By Jo Howarth

Success…that elusive thing. The thing that we all say we want in life and yet, when we talk about success, most of us are talking about money. When we talk about success, most of us are picturing the big house with the flash car and a bank account that overflows with dosh. That was absolutely my view of success for most of my younger years.

But here's what I've learned.

The reason that we want all of those things is because we believe that they will make us happier. We want "success" because we believe we will be happier when we are "successful."

I talk every day in my work about happiness being the most important thing in life because whatever that thing is that we want in life, whatever that level of success is that we desire, what we actually want in the having of it is to feel happier, which, for me, makes happiness the true meaning of success.

Over the years, I have dealt with and overcome much adversity in my life and business. The consistent desire was to feel more content, peaceful, and happy through all of it.

My childhood was ok, not idyllic. I had divorced parents, two siblings, step-parents and a daily dose of anxiety to deal with, not that I knew that's what it was called way back then.

My teens and twenties were filled with the usual angst, with feeling less than the people I was friends with, who seemed to have more money, bigger houses and better families than I did, and with making some really bad choices in romantic relationships, including a hefty dose of emotional abuse.

The biggest hit of all came when my biological dad passed away suddenly from a heart attack when I was 25. He was here one day and gone the next. No rhyme, no reason, no warning, just gone. That was what turned my entire world upside down and inside out. That was the thing that sent me to therapy for the first time in my life.

Therapy is the path that I have been on ever since, on and off. Therapy helped me to start seeing myself and the world around me differently. Therapy helped me put the jigsaw puzzles together so that the picture appeared how I wanted it to. Therapy has helped me, on and off, for the last 25 years. All different types of therapy, and ultimately, it led me to train to become a therapist myself to help people in the way I have been helped in my life. Therapy led me to the discovery that happiness is the most important thing in life, that happiness is what we're all after, even when we tell ourselves that it's the money, the house, the car or the relationship.

When writing this, I am going through my own divorce proceedings. Another learning curve for me, another set of difficulties to move through, more adversity, but adversity is what leads us to happiness. Adversity helps us uncover our strengths and reach out for help with our perceived weaknesses. Adversity is the mud that something truly beautiful can grow from.

Take the example of my dad dying all those years ago. I always describe that as the worst thing that ever happened to me and the best thing that ever happened FOR me. His passing led me to a path I'm unsure I would have otherwise found. There is so much good that has grown out of it, so much beauty that has come into my life as a result, and so much happiness that I have created that wouldn't have been possible without that horrible thing happening in the first place.

So, if adversity leads us to happiness and happiness is the true meaning of success, how do we achieve success?

I follow a simple formula that I share with my clients, and I would love to share it with you now in the pages of this beautiful book.

The first step is awareness. Awareness is the key to life, the universe and everything. The more aware you can be of your thoughts, feelings, beliefs, the stories you tell yourself daily, the people around you, the world around you, and your place in that world, the more you can see, receive, and hold on to those realisations and learnings. How do you increase your awareness of all that? By paying attention. By simply checking in with yourself regularly, asking yourself how you feel right now, asking yourself whether that thought or belief is actually serving you, and taking the time to sit and notice it all going on within and around you.

The next step is allowing and accepting. Accepting wherever you are and whatever you're experiencing in any given moment. The more you move into a state of acceptance, the more you remove that human urge to push against the things you don't want to be happening, and the more you open yourself up to happiness. By allowing yourself to feel however you feel in each of those moments is a key component of that acceptance. Allowing your emotions to be there, allowing them to flow through you, allowing them to move on easily and naturally, allowing yourself to experience them. As human beings, we can find that difficult; we are taught from a young age that certain emotions are "bad" or that we should hide them or not feel them. But all of your emotions are valid, temporary, and transitory if you allow them to be present and then move on.

The third step is appreciation. Practising and cultivating a deep sense of appreciation for yourself, others, the world, and all the happenings, situations, and circumstances. Not pretending everything is rosy when it isn't, not forcing yourself to find the silver lining when it's unbelievably well-hidden, but fostering a genuine sense of appreciation whenever you can will help to soften the blows and expand your experience.

And lastly, love. Ahh, that beautiful feeling. Love in all its forms. Kindness, compassion, romance and straightforward love. Self-love is the most important of all and, again, the thing that most of us struggle with. Showing ourselves the love we so readily dish out to others can be hard, but the more we allow ourselves to experience it, the happier we become.

Success is available to us all because happiness is available to us all. And it doesn't mean you can't still desire the house, the car, the money; it's just about understanding that those things are not what success is……Happiness is.

JULIA JONES
2024

CHAPTER 5

What's Life Without Purpose?

By Julia Jones

Finding myself in between husbands was quite a life-changing experience. Not that I had two husbands, and I was literally in between them. One marriage had ended, and the future was unknown to me!

What happened to me 'in-between' husbands? I hear you cry!

Well, my first recollection of a change in me was a series of discoveries. Here are some of those 'whoooooooa' moments:

- Hair straighteners – the instrument of wonderment creating super sexy hair.
- Anne Summers was an emporium of wonder and merchandise that was not seedy after all!
- Oh, and the best discovery - pubic hair was an optional extra! WOW!

Julia 'the screwed up and poorly' had become Julia, the wife, then Julia, the mother and now…future Julia! which felt liberating and a bit wild!

Having lost over three stone in weight (around 19kg in new world currency), I discovered that I rocked a smart suit and heels, tight jeans, and a t-shirt that did not reach my knees.

It seemed apt to start a new career now that I had suits, heels, thongs, and straight hair!

Can you, dear reader, resonate with the wonderful superhero that is Bridget Jones? Of course you can! I LOVE her, particularly the books. Her desire to find a husband and her adventures really resonate with me.

I was NOT in search of a husband like Briget, however. My adventures were not specific or purposeful. More of a 'bury your head in the sand' and survive day-by-day approach to life, goalless and not understanding why anyone would want to plan their lives out on a to-do list; how boring!

My aimless rambles led me through life's normal difficulties, highs, and lows, through stupidity and misery and, luckily, in a direction that helped me discover 'my purpose in life.'

It was always there; I did not know it existed until I realised I had assembled my very own neon billboard, climbed down the ladder, and stood back to read what it was screaming to me!

Around the same time the billboard started screaming, completely without ceremony, I discovered something else. The ability to use my voice! That might not seem significant, but think about this: You are eating out and are asked, "Is everything okay with your meal?" Fess up, what do you say? You are in conversation with your besties, so you respond, without thinking, "Yes, thanks," do you not?

On a particular day when I was 33, I responded like this to that same question... "if you hadn't walked away before I had time to respond to your question, you would have heard me say that I am really disappointed with this food!" Mic drop! Where had that come from? I hadn't heard HER voice before...it felt A-mazing!

That moment was so significant because I had discovered I had grown emotionally.

Whatever your personal journey is, sometimes you take a significant step towards being the 'Future You.' You will know when you get there, because you will find yourself rolling your eyes heavenwards and hearing the voice in your head saying things like, "I wish I had done this years ago....,"

But we do not because we cannot. We are not ready. My nan would have said, "You can't put an old head on young shoulders."

But WHY can't we? Why can't we help young people better understand that feeling confused, overwhelmed, and misunderstood is okay like there is no purpose to life? THESE THINGS ARE NORMAL IN YOUR TWENTIES. Why do we talk about puberty with such wisdom and gusto when the early twenties are worse! Much, much worse! We expect that our young adults, with child-like emotions and zero experience, can navigate their way in this bat-shit crazy world! For their part, they think they ARE adults and then beat themselves up for not being able to join 'the race', and so they 'fake it until they make it'...or break. I have that T-shirt, but it's a different story!

We, the ones that are now in the bat-shit crazy race of life, haven't done a good enough job on adapting to the way we support our young adults, in my opinion. If we had, we wouldn't be living in a time where every tween, teen and young adult is labelled (and self-labels themselves) as having depression and anxiety.

Please don't shoot me yet. Consider this; some of those feelings we all experience are normal, and different words are helpful to describe a feeling or emotion. If we used other words, we might be able to 'own' our emotions and feelings, try to make sense of them and help ourselves!

There you go – owning it rather than blaming others. Is that a shift for a lot of us? I am not saying it is easy; it is far from it! But instead of "You're making me anxious," I might respond, "Today I am feeling tired and out of control. I do not want to be here; I want to curl up and not participate in the world."

If I go any further, I might land myself in deep water with the professionals.

So, for the professionals, I own every word I write, and you can blame it on my lived experience of being, birthing and working with young people.

Okay, back to me! Remember, I love Bridget, made amazing discoveries, complained in a restaurant, and erected a billboard...

The chances were that I was wearing my best suit and heels when I stood in front of 120 people with my notes trembling between my hands. I had not done anything like this before! I looked a sea of faces thinking 'what do I have to offer you all?'

The brief from my CEO: *"We want you to talk at the conference and enlighten your peers about how you have managed to generate more new business in a recession than they have."*

You see, my numbers had come from nowhere. I was inexperienced compared to my audience; my numbers were not spectacular, and, what's more, I knew that despite my achievement, many of the audience would finish the year with much higher results and commissions than I would. So why me???? When I posed this question to my CEO and manager, the words of praise they used felt like they were blowing smoke up my arse! All I ever did, as far as I was concerned, was to do the job I loved.

I looked down at my hand and began to read from the tiny piece of paper.

Hello mummy,

I missed you today. I am proud of you.

I love you more than chocolate.

Love from

Grace

I went on to talk about a book that I had read. A parable about four mice whose lives changed when someone moved the cheese in their maze to a new location. Finally, I talked loosely about some pretty pie charts with numbers.

My message to the audience? No one told me that focusing on a recession was more important than feeding my kids. Why would I choose to focus on negativity that I had no control over? Why wouldn't my focus be on the things I *could* control – role modelling hard work to my kids so that I could earn more of those little love letters.

The audience were crying when I finished. WOW! What had I done to them?

I realised (sometime later) that my CEO asked me not because of my numbers but because of my 'why.'

My neon billboard says three words. 'Leaving a legacy.'

Being tuned into 'Purpose' does not mean no more fuckups. Mary Poppins and I could not be more different. I want to be remembered for jumping up and down on the bed, spilling wine, being the last person to get the joke, for my bad music, passion, and tenacity.

Around this time, the confusion from my twenties started to make sense. Suppose I had not been stubborn about to-do lists or keeping a diary. In that case, I might have avoided the chaos and high energy I created around myself and reached more of my potential earlier in life.

But I have always taken the longest route, where the 'peaks and troughs' have been more like navigating the journeys between mountains and valleys on ice skates.

I have had an incredible journey, but it only started to come together when the billboard went up.

Without purpose, what is the point of life?

Finding purpose in the early twenties is almost impossible because we do not know it is a 'thing'!

I knew I had to stay alive for my first dog, Casper. He needed me, and I was not going to let him down. I was 26. Then it was the kids.

Without the kids, I am not sure I would have been here today because I cannot think of any other reason to validate my contribution to this world. Everything I have accomplished, from the billboard and standing on that stage to today, has been about me fulfilling my purpose.

At some point, about 10 years ago, another vital life lesson landed. It landed with me in a field surrounded by a herd of horses and is significant enough to mention to you.

"Where do you get your support from Julia?" Was the question asked by my coach? Silence from me while I processed the ridiculous question! What on earth do I need support for? Am I weak?

Why would I burden my friends with my troubles? What craziness would allow me to ask for help? They must have picked up a weakness in me. As my mind raced, I switched my attention to the environment, and what I observed blew my mind.

Five horses stood around me in a circle; I was in the centre. Each one was standing, with their backsides facing me. The image remains with me as one of the most significant lessons of my life.

To this day, I have not felt as alone as I did in those minutes as I realised that my independence, strength, and power were driving people away from me. Until then, I believed I was the only one I could rely on to achieve my purpose.

As the tears fell from my eyes and, I was suffocated with a grief that started in my belly and rose upwards into my chest, I struggled to breathe. One of the horses turned to face me and headed in my direction. I was compelled to seek her out for comfort, and she allowed me to cry into her neck and mane. After a few moments, I felt confused as she walked away from me. It felt like she had come forward to provide a lesson and left when I needed to process what had just happened. How could I have received such comfort? Was this support?

Suffice to say that I do ask for support these days. It has been difficult, but I have better working relationships and much stronger friendships.

Asking for support is different from expecting others to resolve our problems for us. This is an entitlement because we do not own our own challenges. To accept support, we need to appreciate the sentiment of what has been given to us to help us resolve our own issues and be prepared to reciprocate that as often as possible.

I have my own business and will live or die by its success or failure.

Why? Because I want my kids to remember me and to be proud that I tried my best to fulfil my 'Purpose.' A legacy built around my love for them. They will never be rich, but I hope they will remember that I wanted to change as many lives as possible by helping as many people as possible to become the best version of themselves by being self-aware and able to find their purpose.

This year, someone asked me, "What's your contingency plan if the business fails?" I said nothing because I was trying to process why I would need a contingency plan.

When everything about you has always been built around having a purposeful existence and overcoming, not hurdles, but fucking mountains on ice skates, failure is not an option and a contingency plan might be sensible, but then again, people don't really know me or that I now accept support from people I trust these days.

My business is called Altezza People UK. Altezza is Italian for peak, height, and highness. My logo is an image of my daughter and first horse.

We support corporate guests to tap into their peak performance. I have combined my talent for understanding people, gained over decades, with my own life lessons and one final secret ingredient, my own herd of horses. Yes, that personal experience just over a decade ago helped me to link my purpose with support and a new one – passion. I am authentically in the best place in my life ever!

Horses are intuitive and non-verbal and give feedback to unspoken truths. What better way to learn about yourself? I am truly blessed, and so are our guests! I also still travel and work with businesses across the globe because I love to learn about people and how to help them to support themselves.

The best day I could describe these days was when I delivered a self-awareness workshop for a group with my herd of horses. I return home to my family at the end of the day, and they know I have used my talents to serve others.

Do not be too hard on yourselves; be patient and tap into why you do what you do. Your emerging purpose will be there somewhere; you must find it! Look for the gift-wrapped box that sits just above the one that contains your values and just below the one protecting your emotions and feelings. If you need help cutting the ribbon, reach out, I would love to help!

Finally, remember to erect your own billboard with flashing neon lights. Never ever take your focus from it. You will thank me one day!

KERRY TUSCHOFF
2024

CHAPTER 6

The Birth of Me

By Kerry Tuschoff

My success journey actually started when I was 16 years old and watching a Patty Duke movie in which she was giving birth to her baby at home, screaming in agony, and her baby did not survive. Horrified, I swore I would never have children. EVER.

But … Fast forward to 1988, a friend gave birth to her first baby using no medication, no IV, no monitor, no episiotomy, and no operative technology of any kind. She was obviously in a lot of pain, but she was able to give birth naturally, which, at that time in my life, I didn't realise people still did! She had taken a Bradley Method class to prepare for her birth and told me many things she had learned about the body's ability to give birth naturally and without intervention. I was fascinated and began researching childbirth methods since all I had heard about previously was Lamaze.

A "birth junkie" in training: I became "hooked" as I learned about nature's most perfect plan – childbirth. The more I read and studied, the more I knew from somewhere inside that I wanted to be a part of this plan, teaching other women the truth about their abilities to create a better birth. I contacted the group that certifies Bradley Instructors, and they agreed to allow me to take the teacher training even though I had not yet given birth. I excitedly took the course, receiving an invaluable education in natural childbirth, and taught my initial class when I was pregnant with my first baby. I thought I knew a great deal about the body's ability to give birth and women's strength and determination, and that seemed to be enough as I planned for my natural, unmedicated birth centre water birth. **Then I went into labour!**

My first baby's birth: The incredible unstoppable power and wretched pain of a posterior baby for 26 hours of unmedicated terror took its toll, and it took quite a long time to get over the fact that I was more ecstatic to see the anesthesiologist than I was for my baby that was soon to be born! I ended up being transferred from my beloved birth centre to a hospital across the street. I'll never forget the pain, shame and fear that swept through me as I was wheeled outside and across a major street, with everyone staring at me as I screamed with each contraction. An epidural was procured for me and administered by a very sensitive anesthesiologist. After quite a few other tubes, wires, and procedures, I slept for a while, and six hours after my hospital arrival, my baby was pushed and pulled out with the aid of a very strong nurse and a doctor with a vacuum extractor. The loss of my dream, my natural waterbirth, devastated me, and I was overcome with disbelief. Yes, I had my little princess, and she was perfect, but I had dreamed of, planned for, and counted on her birth being the empowering, glorious experience I felt all women deserved. It was the first time I fully realised how intensely powerful the experience of childbirth is for everyone, and it was life-changing for me. It was also the first time I fully understood why people would choose an epidural, and I gained a healthy respect for those who do.

Postpartum Depression and Trauma: Almost immediately after giving birth, I began experiencing deep depression, insomnia, and crying spells. I had spasms of pain up and down my spine, legs, and neck from the epidural, which lasted a long time. I began jumping at noises and being unable to concentrate and sought help from a physician for postpartum depression. I have since learned that many people suffer postpartum depression and even PTSD from the trauma they have suffered during childbirth, and many remain undiagnosed and/or untreated. This has motivated me even further to help find a way **to prevent birth trauma**, and Hypnobabies have been a huge part of that picture for so many people.

My second baby's birth and what it taught me: Four years almost to the day after my daughter was born, I gave birth to my son in a birthing tub at a birth centre after seven hours of very intense labour. Although the physical pain was just as bad as my first baby's birth, the time it lasted was far shorter, and the dynamics of the labour were different. I was amazed, however, at how tremendously painful this labour was, and I was sorely disappointed that, again, my "relaxation" practice had not worked.

During this harrowing second birth, I was writhing in pain, screaming actually, through a particularly gnarly contraction with my husband pushing hard on my back to help alleviate the stabbing pain. My sister was in front of me, holding my hands with hers, and I looked up into her face, which was streaming with tears, and she said, “It should never have to be this hard…” and we cried together. As the pain of that contraction subsided, in my anguish, I realised she was right; that people who wanted an unmedicated birth should never have to suffer like this. I knew right there and then that even if I never had another child (and I did not), I was going to find a way to help others so that childbirth could be the joyous event I knew it could be.

Hypnobirthing? I went online and began a campaign to learn more about hypnosis for childbirth, finding quickly that there were quite a few programs and methods out there. I watched an episode of Dateline NBC on hypnotic childbirth, which showed two women going through their labours calmly and very relaxed, with very little birth pain. That was my goal for my future childbirth students. I contacted a major hypnobirthing organisation to begin my journey towards it with their Practitioner Training. I took their 2-day Introduction to Hypnosis class and the 2-day Training course. I arrived at that training course extremely excited and thrilled since I thought I had finally found a way that my wonderful, dedicated, natural childbirth students would no longer have to suffer. I saw “hypno-birth” videos of women labouring seemingly with little pain, using only this organisation’s techniques. I was sure my future “hypnobirthing” students would look and feel just like that, and I already had my business cards and letterhead done, a website and other preparations.

Teaching: I began teaching my hypnosis-birthing class with passion, enthusiasm, and the comforting belief that these students were the luckiest ones alive; surely they would have no drugs and little pain as they laboured and gave birth to their babies. There were five couples in my first class, and I showed them the exact hypno-materials and information I was taught to teach, which included a book, one light hypnosis audio track and a 15-minute birth affirmations audio track. A few handouts and two hypnosis scripts were included. I added only a bit about nutrition to the class and excitedly waited for my “Hypno-moms” to give birth.

The first “hypno-birth”: I attended my first hypnobirthing student’s birth at a birth centre as her doula, and I became very distressed to find that she could not stay relaxed or comfortable by herself, even in early labour at home using her “hypnobirthing”. She went to the birth centre and progressed from 3cm to 10cm in three hours, which was amazing, but she was suffering quite a lot of pain as she entered active labour, and nothing we did or tried helped her. Her transitional period was only about an hour, but she was extremely miserable during it, and I was at a loss to comfort her since she had given up on the hypnosis and tried to "relax". She finally gave birth and was reasonably pleased with her experience since she said her hypnosis "helped at the beginning". However, this was not what I had envisioned for my students. I convinced myself that this birthing experience was just a fluke and that the next birth would be much better.

More births as a doula: Each of my "hypno-birth" students' births that I attended after that however, just seemed to get worse instead of better, with the exception of only one of my students who said, "It was manageable." I was in contact by then with several fellow hypno-birth practitioner trainees who lamented that they were having the same results with their students and didn't know how to help them.

The moment I knew I had to create something "different": I taught two "hypno-birth" classes this way (10 couples total), and the births were almost all the same. The last one was the one that changed my life. I attended this woman's birth as her doula, and she was clearly in agony and feeling misled, crying out, cursing me and suffering greatly. I cried all the way home and swore that either I would stop teaching childbirth education at all or I would find a way that my students would be able to be successful in their efforts to have a much more accessible, much more comfortable and fear-free birthing.

I did not stop teaching.

Deep, Somnambulistic Hypnosis: It was clear to me that if I was going to continue teaching hypnosis for childbirth, I needed to know much more about hypnosis itself and how to help my students with personal issues and hypnotic depth problems, as well as find some excellent birth hypnosis scripts. A local hypnotherapist allowed me to sit in on a few hypnosis classes, and only then did I really realise how much I still needed to learn about **therapeutic hypnosis** and its uses for actually eliminating pain. Immediately, I took a course in hypnosis and hypnotherapy, which helped me tremendously to understand how and why a deeper form of hypnosis could work for childbirth. I could now teach my students successful pain elimination, not pain management! The same kind of deep, somnambulistic hypnosis techniques produce "hypno-anaesthesia", which allows medical and dental patients to undergo surgery and other procedures without medical anaesthesia (due to severe allergies). **I was elated!**

YES! The day that I found **Gerald Kein's Painless Childbirth Program** is one of joyful commemoration for me since so many missing pieces were found. Master hypnotist Gerald Kein had actually sat down with a group of pregnant women and asked them what they wanted and needed for a comfortable natural birth. Their candid answers gave him the information he needed to create a hypnosis program that women could easily use to eliminate pain and fear from childbirth yet be able to move around freely during labour, eat and drink, and communicate their needs to others. **Fantastic!**

Creating Hypnobabies: I then began creating Hypnobabies, a complete childbirth program that used Gerald Kein's main Painless Childbirth techniques (with his permission – he was thrilled!) along with several other great ideas and concepts. I also decided to do what Gerald Kein had done and listen to our students so that Hypnobabies could include even more techniques, cues, and "tools" for a more comfortable birth.

Beginning to teach: As I taught my first Hypnobabies classes, I noticed that my hypno-couples may have arrived in Class #1 feeling sceptical and fearful to various degrees; they all left Class #5 so confident and free of fear, having seen the fruits of their practice and work at home, in class sessions and in our class's Birth Rehearsal. They needed to learn how to take responsibility for their birthing, so I included **birthing choices,** risks, benefits and alternatives to common hospital interventions. This has become invaluable to those who want to enter labour confidently and leave it in peace. Adding excellent nutrition and exercise information, as well as stages of labour, fetal positioning, avoiding back labour, and other important issues, rounded out Hypnobabies and helped make it successful. Knowledge is power!

Healing Births: I soon realised how regenerative a Hypnobabies birth can also be for those who have had a difficult birth experience; a true Healing Birth. Since childbirth is a huge event in each person's life, and most of us will remember every detail of each baby's birth, these amazing people have given themselves a precious gift when they choose to prepare for childbirth this way. Every time a Hypnobabies student has a great birth experience, she can also go on and teach others (including attending birth professionals) how sweet and lovely childbirth can be instead of the nightmare tales usually told of “labour”. Another Hypno-baby is born more comfortably, without violence, without hearing its mother scream. Gentle birthing at its best. **This is ‘it!’**

As I have evolved as a childbirth educator, author, doula and lecturer, I’ve found that each person’s strength and power actually come from within as they give birth, and we all need to learn how to tap into it and use it purposefully. These special people who have stepped “out of the box” to prepare for birth in such a different way and give their babies the gift of a gentle start in life **inspire me … every day. That is my success, and it is glorious!**

"

I have a firm belief in the ability and power of women to achieve the things they want to achieve.

ELEANOR ROOSEVELT

KEZZABELLE AMBLER

2024

CHAPTER 7

Mermaid, Angel, Fairy Poet

By Kezzabelle Ambler

I was born in Tripoli, Libya, in the 60s, a middle child of an older brother and a younger sister. I have always had an affinity to water, fearlessly crawling into the sea as a baby, repeatedly taken out, only to crawl in again, like a pull-back toy. I was quietly independent and insistent on feeding myself, leading to my nickname Messy Min. I explored my surroundings by scooting myself along on my bum on the marble floors in the Liverani Villas on the outskirts of Tripoli. Our house boy Hasan (who helped when my dad worked away) often proudly pushed the pale, unusual blonde bundle along the streets in a high-sided Silver Cross pram (that my mum insisted on shipping over for protection from scorpions that scuttled loudly across the floor) My dad was in the Military Police, during the reign of King Idris', where the gold-domed palace's immaculate lawns were sprinklered daily, whilst the people suffered water and electricity shortages and women gave birth in the streets until the revolt and Gaddafi came. The Brits left, my family included, and returning to England, I cried, missing and asking for Hasan.

Back in Rushden, Northamptonshire, my grandma, on first sight of me, said, 'Has she got worms?!' I was shy and thin with translucent skin, ice blue eyes and snow white hair but also had a determined 'knew what I liked and didn't like' attitude, which included not liking pasteurised milk, tea and many traditional English foods, much too the annoyance of my grandparents.

My parents separated shortly after our return to the UK, and my father left to adventure around Europe to spend his new loves' inheritance; family life was not for him. My single mum brought us up with discipline and love; she was a devoted socialist and took the three of us and the pushchair leafleting for the Labour Party around the town; we sang songs and pretended to march to keep warm.

She was a big supporter of the National Health Service, often quoting Aneurin Bevan; even on her last day on this earth in December '22, she repeated, 'free at the point of need, it's so important to fight for our NHS'. She often quoted Shakespeare too; she loved words and was suitably impressed when she heard me, age five, reading to my siblings, 'The woodcutter and his wife....'

I loved words, read a lot and played many word games with my grandma and grandpa Lewin (I recall he sent poems and letters of complaint to national newspapers and was very proud when they printed them). My grandma often read Rupert Bear stories to us on sleepovers; maybe that's where my love of rhyme was planted.

We lived in poverty when my dad left, but my mum was proud; friends brought around rabbits shot in the fields (she soaked them in salt to make the meat look paler, telling us it was chicken). She would ask the butcher for bones for the dog. We didn't even have a dog, but she'd add the bones to vegetables to sustain us. She confessed in later years that she'd tiptoed out at night in slippers with a pillowcase to steal coal from the train station to keep us warm. I told these tales many years later, in 2020, just before performing my poem 'Prejudge' at a mosque in Leamington Spa. I was headlining a 'Poets For Peace' event. I needed to get the attention of a room full of two hundred Muslim men who, indeed, could have easily prejudged the blonde, curvaceous poetess in front of them; once they'd heard part of my story and the poem, they were totally listening.

Prejudge

Summarise the projected image.
First impressions, public outer disguise.
Judging, not exploring the inner story
behind the stranger's eyes.

Naturally, we're drawn to certain people
that we feel most comfortable around,
want to belong, connect, to fit.
Social community, common ground.

Preconceptions, distorted perceptions.
Prejudging, of that we're all guilty.
Typecast and titles given
'goth', 'chav', 'dumb blonde' 'LGBT'.

Eligibility and participation
of pecking orders, clans or class.
Reject being defined, unlock the box,
and disassociate from this farce.

Open eyes, hearts and minds.
Embrace and encourage inclusivity.
Rally our rich mix of differences
incite a harmonious society.

Kezzabelle Ambler © 5.10.2016 Commissioned for National Hate Crime Week 2016 by Northamptonshire Rights and Equality Council **https://youtu.be/dIlc5h42xjY?si=tZP-iaGFrLciuKSg**

A massive transformation in my life came at the age of seven when we moved to Kettering; what a life education change that was with an inspirational teacher called Mr Mathers determined to find a strength or talent in each and every child; I learnt so much from him and at home too, as we'd moved into a flat above my mum's first independent fashion boutique in Northants called 'Honeyspot Boutique' (her parents lent her the rent deposit). Whilst my mum ran the business my siblings and I were taken care of by a host of bohemian and artistic childminders, who really expanded our creative minds and view of life.

As a teenager, my confidence grew. Sitting on the flat's window sills high over the town, I would people watch on busy Saturdays, wondering where the people had been and where they were going; what were they thinking? My siblings sometimes said,' You think too much or 'You're too sensitive'; as a teenager, wanting to fit in and belong is often all you wanted. Now, my alternative quirky 'thinking outside the box' observations shine through my poetry alongside my curiosity and questioning. When I was old enough, I helped in my mum's boutique on Saturdays; all the time, I watched how she served and her love of the people who crossed her path; she taught me to ask, 'How can I help you', and that has stayed with me ever since. She gave time to people whether they came in to see the latest styles she'd bought that week in London or if they popped in for a chat and to ask for help or advice. There was a lot of partying at the flat, but although surrounded by drink and drugs, I was never that interested (I found out 40 years later from an old lady in my church home group that she and the church had prayed regularly for the teenagers in the centre of town, concerning drugs. Coincidence or God-incidence!)

I had pre-show nerves at 14 and 15 years old, modelling and dancing in fashion shows that my mum ran around the county. Still, I always had a wonderful natural high afterwards. There were many late-night rehearsals and quick clothes changes; I observed my mum's hard work and patience in handling different people and egos, ensuring everything ran smoothly; her mantra was always, 'Love is the answer', which we still repeat. I watched and learned from her use of words in her descriptive talks on the mic of shapes, colours, and cuts of fabrics, sharing 'dress for the occasion' advice. She cleverly raised awareness of the boutique and its fashions while raising funds for local charities. She had many fun and innovative ways of drawing attention to the boutique. She was always in the local Evening Telegraph. I was five years younger than most of the models, but after most shows, the girls and my mum would sneak me in with them to the local nightclub, where my love of music and dancing grew. I'll never forget a guy coming up to me and saying, 'I want what you're on' he thought I was high on something; I wasn't. I was just loving life, the music, dancing and drinking fizzy pop! Still, to this day, people often think I'm drunk or on something when I'm just enjoying life to its full and sharing my energy and smiles.

At nearly sixteen, I worked in a beach restaurant in the South of France for two long summers with my brother, studying business, English, shorthand and typing between college. It was an exciting and nerve-wracking adventure to travel alone for the first time abroad, but once there, I adored sleeping by the sea in a beach hut, enjoying my mermaidiness (made-up word), swimming in the sea daily, sometimes windsurfing and water skiing after long days of preparing French platters for the sunbathers and windsurfers. I learned so much about different cultures, languages, food, and lifestyles in those two summers in the seventies. **https://youtu.be/h44PD5jM8c8?si=2mGTJ1r9-fsSeoU4**

Young Woman by the Sea

Exams completed, awaiting college,
almost 16 years old,
I travelled alone
on an old coach to Nice.
Churney nervous tummy,
I arrived, greeted by sunshine,
a smiling stranger, and my brother,
both dressed in baggy shorts and flip-flops.

I received a warm, friendly,
French family beach restaurant welcome.
Dressed and tasty Mediterranean food,
oil, wine and water.
Introduced to the tiny kitchen,
my new workplace for the next 3 months,
taught to make salade noises, tarte au citron
and platters of charcuterie.

My small preparation worktop
was right next to a large gaping, wooden framed space
(occasionally used as a window)
Slap bang on a sandy beach
I overlooked parasoled sunbathers,
windsurfers and swimmers playing
on lazy turquoise waves,
where daily we drew fresh mussels in small nets.

I was shown my 'room',
a basic bare beach hut
with just a sun lounger mattress on the floor.
My bag and cuddly toy dog 'Spud' by my pillow,
I lay my head to dream.
Open minded to living this new experience
I fell asleep, soothed by the gentle rhythmic tidal
lapping at the water's edge.

Kezzabelle Ambler©19.10.2016

I fell in love at sixteen and married my first love at nineteen; in my twenties and thirties, we had 5 children; I was a school governor, ran mums and tot's groups, and later ran youth groups and organised and ran live music events and annual festivals for under 18s. My partner and I ran our T-shirt printing business, using our print factory to fulfil designs and prints all over the world.

I remember writing my first poem aged 12 and a half. I could hear the rest of the family watching Monty Python on the TV in the living room, and I wanted to finish my homework to join them. My colourful, slightly crazy poem about jesters and circuses was graded A+, which my literature teacher then crossed out and wrote underneath, "Is this all your own work?" I haven't written another poem for over thirty years. I often remind people of this story and the power of the spoken word. One of my first poems as an adult in 2006 was 'Complicated Love'. It was so revealing to me that I hid it. Writing again made me notice a lot outwardly and inwardly; it revealed how unhappy I felt in my relationship.

After three years of trying to save my marriage with counselling, prayer and making changes, I continued pouring my heart out onto paper; I was being totally honest with myself on many levels for the first time in a very long time, and we subsequently separated. Those raw emotions and observations of life became the basis for my early poetry as I tried to work life out.

My debut performance and inspiration for my name 'Kezzabelle' came from my first gig in the vaudeville Playhouse Theatre Northampton between burlesque and belly-dancing sets whilst they changed. The audience responded positively to my poems; they even asked if I had a book for sale! I continued reading at open mic nights around Northamptonshire to learn my craft. A year later, my first booklet 'Truly Me' was published, which I took back to the Playhouse Theatre when booked for two more paid slots. Two years later, my second, slightly tongue in cheek, 'Kezzabockerglory (with extra sauce)', was released and sold at festivals, cabaret nights and spoken word events.

I wrote the poem 'Three Wishes' as I swam, jumping in and out of the pool to scribble down my ideas on receipts and scraps of paper before I forgot them. I often wore a tutu and wings when asking the audience to think of three wishes, revealing most of what the audience was thinking in my performance, earning me the name 'Fairy Poet' in Nottingham and further afield. Sometimes I was introduced on stage as 'Mistress of Mischief and Wordsmith Wench.

Https://youtu.be/CXRFWaN5iS4?si=t6vGiLkkjvgOiJ1u

Three Wishes

I'm the fairy of life
come to grant you three wishes,
think carefully, think hard,
dig deep; life's wonderfully delicious.

Something pops in your head,
oh, to be a stone lighter
but if I click my fingers now
would your life actually be brighter?

Holidays, cocktails lying by the pool,
buy the latest gadget telly,
eat out more, damn, lost my last wish
as I look down at my belly.

Oooh to have **'her'** right now,
that girl with an extraordinary bust
but what happens then
after that moment of lust?

A big house? A fast car?
Roof down, shades, cool guy
but to get where faster
and exactly why?

I'm the fairy of life
come to sprinkle some magic,
be careful what you wish for
lives may become tragic.

Health, Wealth and Happiness
throw me that easy cliché.
Look inside, what fills you,
what's important to you each day?

Do you wish for more money?
It sometimes means strife
how many possessions do we need,
do they stress-free your life?

What we want, what we need,
and are they the same?
We can't take it with us
so what's there to gain?

Busy, buzzing about
chasing that money,
whilst missing our blessings,
life's God-given honey.

As the fairy of life
I see your talents; start giving,
steer to that high-on-life feeling
and really start living.

I'm the fairy of life
come to grant you three wishes.
Make a difference in a good way,
start with, 'love', 'hugs' n 'kisses'

Kezzabelle Ambler ©15.5.2013

My third book 'All the Loves' led to more performances and local radio interviews. To share my knowledge and inspiration learnt over five years of attending numerous and varied writing sessions, I wrote and prepared a six-week course to run 'Weaving Words', a weekly creative writing workshop around my dining room table; I served different teas in small individual teapots, home-made vegan fruity flapjack, nuts and fruits. There was a real warmth and community feel around that table, with people of different ages, backgrounds and abilities coming together to express, heal and play with words. At the end of the course, many Word Weavers didn't want to leave and continued attending my workshops for eight years until 2022. We continued through lockdown via Zoom (which was a lifesaver for us all).

The connection and growth I saw in the people who came was incredible and very moving; I felt and feel privileged to run them. Some of the reviews brought me to tears; Tony Roberts said, *"Kezzabelle does so much to enrich my life and the lives of others too. We all need those who are a drink of water in the desert. Thank you."*

I used my 10 years experience of youth work to run 'Weaving Words Youth' too, working with many children in and out of school, some with additional needs, curating bespoke writing projects in Northants for children and young people, playing a pivotal role in winning a Community Award for Creative Writing at the Montagu Monuments project under the Northamptonshire Heritage Forum Awards.

I think my genuine passion for encouraging others to be creative is a large part of my success; you can feel the love in the room in the weekly workshops in 'Johnny's Happy Place' in mental health wards and in Well-being Centres with vulnerable adults in the community. It's so rewarding, I love it.

But my biggest successes in life, my pride and joy are my five kids and five grandchildren whom I read stories to, dance with and laugh with, whom I love dearly, remembering 'we'll get through this together' the words I whispered as I held my kids when we lost our first grandson, nephew, son, Chayse; never forgetting my mum's mantra 'love is the answer'. x

A Weaving Words Experience

I'd love to encourage and inspire you
to express your creativity,
you're worth some quality time and space,
to spill your words, feel free to be.

All you need is a clear page
or your favourite device,
a safe place to empty your mind,
let your pen become a tool for life.

Inhale nature, art, music and memories,
start by scribbling; just let go.
No comparisons to others,
no wrong nor right, allowed to flow.

It's your time to tell your story,
let your thoughts and imaginings take flight,
enjoy a Weaving Words Experience,
simply 'watch, pause and write'.

Ever expanding my experience and looking for ways to communicate with my mixed audiences, I recorded my fourth book, 'When You Say Yes' onto Cd. Kenneth J Nash was so impressed by my collection of poems that he signed me to the 'Old Hotel Records label' and assisted me with other CD releases.

Around this time, I had a life-changing spiritual experience; I was dressed as a fisherman, holding a rod, wearing a flat cap, and sitting for a dozen artists in Oak Apple Art studios. Being still for 45 minutes takes me into many beautiful meditative states. This particular time, I saw myself surrounded by light, looking like a mermaid, angel, or fairy dancing with the fish in the sea; it was joyous but quickly changed to heavy blinking eyes, slow and hard, like a lighthouse. I was frantically trying to save the fish from being dashed upon the rocks; I came out of the meditation with tears streaming down my face with a room full of artists and easels, looking very perplexed.

Just before I opened my eyes, I felt and heard the words, 'There's important work to be done' From that point on, I decided to go completely freelance. It was a challenging first year, but I haven't looked back; that 'when you say yes attitude' helped me so much, even getting me a small speaking part in the Alan Moore film 'The Show' with an Equity Card and an incredible new experience under my belt (you'll spot me in a sparkly green corset, a massive bright pink wig as madam juror).

I launched my fifth book, 'Permission To Speak'; I had found my voice and wanted to help others find theirs, too. Writing my feelings, thoughts and observations onto the page helped me through a divorce, a breakdown and some very challenging life situations. My pen has become a 'tool for life' which is why I'm so passionate to help others do the same and have seen many life-changing results.

With the theme of 'Voice' through the three rounds of Bardic Trials, I was voted the 11th Bard of Northampton in 2021. My poem 'Kintsugi Love Repairs' was written to help the people of Northamptonshire pull together after lockdown, join our cracks and flaws, and embrace the art of learning about our precious life scars. It was a privilege to work with Hope Northampton in that 'one year and a day' working with people with addictions in the community and working as an eco-therapist on the land, learning all the way.

I feel so blessed and grateful for the successes that have grown over 14 years since starting to write again as an adult. I am especially proud of my sixth book and audio download, 'Permission To Love Yourself' written before, during and after the lockdown from 2019 to 2023, published by 'Lexical Ninjas'. I'm so excited to take this collection as a one-woman show, backed with film and stage sets, to connect and release our audience's emotions. The shows are being opened by powerful singers, musicians and artists. One of my ultimate goals is to take 'A Weaving Words Experience' to reach and bless as many people as possible, so my team and I are coordinating workshops to be delivered in every town and city into mental health wards and well-being centres we visit as we tour. I would never have expected my creative writing workshops to grow from that small group around my dining room table from strength to strength in person and online, and now filmed workshops are being made into an app too so that it's accessible to all, no matter what ability or time zone, huzzzahhh.

Such exciting times ahead with a lot of hard work, too, curating and collaborating, creating, coordinating and hosting bespoke 'Forget-Me Not Day' retreats, festivals, performances and speaking events. I thank God daily, am prayerfully grateful, and am listening and being guided on this interesting and challenging life path that completely changed at age forty-seven.

Let's take our energy and love of words and people and keep learning, serving and blessing as we go. Let's never give up; everything is possible when you listen to your gut instinct/ God instinct.

That shy little girl now openly shares life experiences to make a difference, connecting through her poetry ranging from sassy, sensual, spiritual, raw, marvellous and sometimes downright naughty.

“

Women who support, uplift and encourage other women without fear of competition, are the most confident women in the world.

JACQUELINE KING

LENORA SCURRY
2024

CHAPTER 8

Weighted Down

By Lenora Scurry

I was born in 1961, and grew up in Lexington, Kentucky. My parents divorced when I was one, and I was raised by my mother. She was a single parent to me and my five siblings, three brothers and two sisters. I was the youngest but definitely not the favourite of the bunch and my momma never tried to pretend otherwise.

One of my earliest memories is of mom looking at a photograph of me and one of my brothers, and saying, "That would have been a great photo, if only you weren't so fat". At just four years old, those words made me feel bad about myself and it got worse from there. Every Christmas, Thanksgiving, or family dinner, mom would humiliate me. Accusing me of piling too much on my plate, telling everyone "I couldn't stop eating". It got to where I would hide in my room every holiday.

The thing is, when I look back at photos of me from that time I wasn't fat at all. I had breasts, a round bottom and thicker thighs than may have been fashionable, but I was not fat!

With an adult's perspective I can now see that my mother had her own demons when it came to eating, food, and body image. She was slender and wanted me to take after her, but she maintained her weight by throwing up after every meal and had an unhealthy relationship with ex-lax that promised to "keep off the pounds". These days we would say she suffered from bulimia and body dysmorphia but in the 1960s she was by no means the only woman to fall into the cycle of pills and purging to keep the weight off.

The constant bullying about my weight led, almost inevitably, to a cycle of binge eating from around the age of nine. When mom wasn't around, I would eat what I wanted and the weight piled on. Even a humiliating visit to a Weight Watcher's meeting with my mother didn't help, if anything it exacerbated my binge eating. Being paraded in front of a roomful of women while hearing my mom describe me as an embarrassment who only wanted to eat, was definitely not what an already unhappy child needed to hear.

Food became my only friend for a long, long time.

I slimmed down in my late teens and early twenties and despite some extremely traumatizing events I married in 1987 and gave birth to a beautiful baby girl. My weight remained pretty stable until my daughter was about six years old, her father and I divorced but I rebuilt us a life in another county and we were doing fine until my daughter was molested, in of all places a church.

My world came tumbling down and once again I turned to food as my saviour. We lived on takeouts and fast food and I began binge eating again…

My weight rocketed to a whopping 401 lbs. I looked and felt awful, and I was ashamed of letting myself get to this state, but with all the other things going on in my life, my weight was not the top priority.

All the excess weight began to cause me serious health problems, and I was put on a multitude of medications, including ones for Type 2 Diabetes. But instead of helping, they made me sicker. My hair was falling out, I was depressed, and it felt as if I was trapped inside a dark tunnel with no possibility of escape.

It wasn't until the birth of my first grandchild in 2010 that things changed. I call him my Guardian Angel; he brought the light back into my life and gave me a reason to live. I didn't want to be a fat grandmother who couldn't play with her grandkids without getting out of breath and exhausted. It was time to do something about losing the weight…and keeping it off.

I began a journey of self-discovery. Spirit spoke to me, saying, "YOU CAN DO THIS. YOU'VE BEEN DEPENDING ON OTHERS YOUR WHOLE LIFE TO HELP YOU. THIS IS YOUR

JOURNEY AND WHEN YOU TAKE CONTROL OF YOUR JOURNEY, YOU'RE GOING TO FIGURE IT OUT".

From that day on, I stopped blaming my mother, took responsibility for my actions, and learned to set boundaries. I found an amazing program called Trauma Recovery Therapy, watched motivational videos, read self-help books, and went to networking events that focused on well-being.

I discovered juicing and lost 22 lbs on a 22-day juice diet, and felt better than I had in years. Low carb came next, and I lost another 40lb. Each time a diet felt like a chore, I tried something new and the pounds continued to drop. But I wasn't building a healthy relationship with food, far from it, and "fad diets" are rarely sustainable for long.

I'm now down to 200 lbs and would like to drop another 60lb, but I now realize there are no quick fixes to losing weight! Pills, potions, drinks, fad diets can only go so far, what is required is a new mindset, and it has to become your lifestyle. I know it seems daunting, but it is so worth it. It's taken me years to reach the point where when the "cookie jar calls" I have the strength to resist, and there are still times when I crave sugar and fast food, but I know that long term health and wellness feels far better than a quick food fix.

I have also had to learn forgiveness – for both my younger self who used food as a prop and to fill the lonely empty void inside, and for my mother who set me down the path of worrying about my weight.

One of my favourite quotes is, "healing isn't easy, but it's beautiful on the other side". If you have a problem with food, be it anorexia, binge eating, bulimia, or you just have a problem with your weight, I want you to know you've got this. Never give up on yourself. It's a moment by moment process. And if I can do it, you can do it.

LISA POGSON
2024

CHAPTER 9

Power of Connection

By Lisa Pogson

I have always been grateful for everything I have, and being a successful woman means showing Gratitude and having the confidence to move forward. I use any opportunity to meet new people, challenges, and open doors. It is said that as 'one door closes, another one opens' and I have often been curious to look into all of them; they can lead you to another connection and tell a new story.

We were lucky growing up; we had family and friends around us.

Simple things made me smile, and still do. Mum always taught us that manners cost nothing and 'Please and Thank You' comes as quickly to me as breathing. We never had lots of spare money; Mum always said we were clean and tidy and polite and that keeping a roof over our heads was always important. They are the fundamentals of my world right there.

When we were young, my Mum, Dad, and the rest of our family had a hard work ethic. Dad worked all over the country as a Lift Engineer and he spent his weekends tinkering with the cars to get to the next place. He gave me a wanderlust for travelling around, as he worked from Scotland to Portsmouth and everywhere between. He had been an older apprentice, learning the trade, and Mum was our base at home and I am so grateful for the love of books that Mum fostered in us.

She would lose herself in a book – still does! We could talk, and she would be following a story and not hear us, usually in the world of Catherine Cookson back then. I share a Kindle library with her now, as well as many books. This love of stories meant regular visits to our local library with my Mum, Aunty and cousins. In spring, that meant a walk through a little wood of bluebells.

Even in a built-up Council house suburb, I remember we had lots of green space around us; Wincobank Hill Fort and Firth Park. If I close my eyes, I can smell those woods now. I still have a love for the wood and of bluebells. These visits meant that we had a constant supply of books, something that I am really grateful for and has made me a keen supporter of libraries to this day. Books that are free to read means education is open to all.

I often read to my younger brother at bedtime and we'd ride the wave of imagination. Books, indeed stories, are my passion. One of my many stories of connection came when I met a travelling storyteller with a suitcase of dreams, who was my new friend, Deborah Bullivant, an ex-Head Teacher turned Founder of a growing literacy charity for children based in Rotherham, working across Yorkshire and beyond. She spun a yarn that wound me in and I am happy to say that I became a Trustee of that charity over nine years ago. I am also Chair for the charity Grimm & Co which will open in 2024 in the charity's new home.

The team literally changed lives, one story at a time. I have seen the profound effect on a child's confidence when being there for a short time. One of the small things they do is to collect books donated in the 'Forgotten Library' and give them to children (and some adults) who may not be able to afford books.

They work with schools and parents, look after children and work alongside the libraries too. It is truly wonderful. Just one example of the Power of Connection and I am grateful for all the doors it has opened to me, the people I have met and the places I have been.

I left school at 16, and all I wanted to do was earn money. Much to my Dad's dismay, I went on what was then a YTS, also thought of as slave labour at the time. I was so grateful to be accepted at a small training provider in Sheffield and was paid whilst I learnt. I started work in an ace architectural practice in Paradise Square, Sheffield and never looked back. Again, the people I met, some of whom I still know today who are strong connections, always amaze me.

They say that there are six degrees of separation and maybe just three degrees in Sheffield – the Outdoor City is like a village. I love it and am so proud to be from here.

South Yorkshire is my base, and I have lived in Rotherham longer. Now our business is there, though it works successfully in London, Thames Valley, and places all over the country. Our company helps to support this region in its small way. The people here are down-to-earth, no-nonsense, heart on their sleeve and say it really as it is – whether you want to hear it or not!

I was so grateful for the business community there, too, that welcomed me as the first female President of the Barnsley & Rotherham Chamber in 2016. I had the most amazing years there as President-Elect, President and Past President. Nine years, alongside Chief Executive Andrew Denniff and the team.

My legacy was supporting changes to the finances and fostering an accurate recognition of the Power of Connection, deeds, not words! Connectivity, Collaboration and Confidence are key to the Chamber Network. It can be so strong and a place to be signposted to someone who can help and support you grow. However, it is important to recognise that connections will not always work for you; they may know someone who can help you in a myriad of other ways though.

I attended an event where Karren Brady was speaking a few years ago. I can't even remember the Conference, but she was headlining. I think she had just become a Baroness. I have followed her career... Same age as me, born the same week as me. Another woman working in a male-dominated industry – a football manager of all things, when I used to be a keen football supporter.

The stand out from the speech for me was when she said someone had once told her that as a leader, you often have to choose between 'Courage and Comfort'. It really stuck in my head. As a Manager, Director, Chair and even as a Mum, in my view, one of the toughest roles, I have found that my courage is sometimes lacking in tough situations.

Lack of sleep and anxiety are things I learned to control as a young person. As an older person with a likely high-functioning ADHD diagnosis, I have struggled with this. Decisions made on a lack of sleep or when you know you are making a life-changing decision for someone, maybe giving them feedback or an outcome that you know they will not like. It can be tough. That is the hardest part of anything I ever have to do. I am an overthinker, and I sometimes have to break that cycle.

The only thing that helps, and it has taken me a long time to learn this, is to sit back and be grateful for being in the role, being in the moment, and having the ability to make those decisions. Be Confident. Be Grateful.

Be YOU.

This year, I will be supporting a small project that I started in 2017 at Grimm & Co., collecting people's favourite quotations that have helped them at their best or worst of times. A Collaboration with all my Connections, which I am truly grateful to have. A couple of my favourites are below. So, small steps can go a long way. Push open a few doors and see what is inside – you can always leave them ajar for others and move forward.

Happy International Women's Day 2024!

"I've learned that people will forget what you said and did but never how you made them feel."

Maya Angelou

"We keep moving forward, opening new doors and doing new things, because we're curious, and curiosity keeps leading us down new paths"

Walt Disney.

"Choose courage over comfort because you can't have both."

Brene Brown

“

What the world needs is more women who have quit fearing themselves and started trusting themselves. What the world needs is masses of women who are entirely out of control.

GLENNON DOYLE

MARIE-LOUISE O'NEILL
2024

CHAPTER 10

The Pursuit of Business 'Appiness'

By Marie-Louise O'Neill

What words come to mind when you think of your business or life? Do any of them include the words 'joy' or 'flow'? Probably not for most people.

I've often likened running my business to riding an extreme roller coaster. In the years since I set up my graphic design business in 2016, there have been some highs and lows and plenty of 'meh' moments (and months). The hard times haven't been only at the beginning when starting out.

Looking back over the last year and earlier, I've realised that there was a big disconnect between the plans I'd set in January and what's been achieved in December. There was also the skewed timescales from how long I thought I would take to achieve those milestones compared to reality.

The main reasons (excuses) were not time or money... although those are common surface reasons for lots of people. My smorgasbord of setbacks were more rooted in mindset such as:

- Procrastination and overthinking.

- Imposter syndrome and negatively comparing myself to others.

- Lack of motivation manifested as days of inaction and inability to do much of anything.

As someone who's invested in various types of coaching over the years, I had enough self-awareness to identify and understand the reasons holding me back. But knowing what to do and taking action are very different things. It took me a frustratingly long time before I could reach out for support that would help me propel forward again.

The virality of social media and the mental hit of the pandemic combined with the general state of the economy have created a perfect storm for us to feel more isolated and alone than ever. This is my quick reminder that what you see on your pal's social media is not the whole picture. It's the highlight reel of the best bits of their life. It's still not the whole story, even when they share a post about their rubbish day or ill health. Many fall into the trap of unfairly comparing our lives with others and judging ourselves harshly if we feel we're not up to scratch.

To put this into perspective for myself, when I fall into that comparison trap, I remember not sharing all aspects of my life on social media. While I'm not afraid to be real or vulnerable when the time is right or when chatting one-on-one, I post the positives, highlights, and fun stuff online. Do you do the same?

We're all dealing with the day-to-day grind, worries and housework and don't need or want to share all that publicly. I don't want to whine about my own problems, but honestly, during the last seven years of running my business, there've been plenty of personal problems in the background that drained my mood, energy and motivation. There's been long-term financial worries, repeated job insecurity for my husband, making ends meet with only me as the 'breadwinner', my husband being diagnosed with a chronic health condition and marital issues that led to a year of counselling. Unsurprisingly, I've yet to post any of these topics on Facebook!

As a quick side note, if you're someone who shares the good, the bad, and the ugly on your social feed, that's your choice. I don't think it's wrong to share all, and many of my connections share that side of what they're going through. It's just not something I've personally done or felt comfortable doing, especially when it's affected my husband or us as a family.

I'm pleased to say that although it's been a tough few years, it's not been bad all of the time, and some of those issues I mentioned are a lot better now. I can happily report back that the couples counselling was successful - just in time for the first lockdown in March 2020! And we're still going strong today. My husband's health is stable, and he now has a good quality of life. The other headaches are still a work in progress but are generally improving, too. I'm feeling positive about my future.

With such long periods of shit hitting the fan, it's no wonder my mental health and mindset were affected. I'm sure you've experienced life-changing events that also shake things up and hit you hard.

So, what can we do when life gives us lemons?

First, I want to tell you about a couple of techniques you need to be wary of and use cautiously.

1: Positivity

You might be thinking that's a bit of a strange one to be wary of. Ironically, I consider myself a positive person. When I make a mistake, or something happens, I try to take a mental step back and see what I can learn from the situation. I focus on working on the solution to get out of the problem.

What I mean specifically is 'toxic positivity'. This is when you're so determined to be positive and to have everything sunshine and roses that you end up deluding yourself or burying the underlying issue. The other side is not allowing yourself the opportunity or space to sit and feel your true emotions in a situation.

I speak with experience about this toxic positivity. Since working for myself, I have hit burnout on two or three occasions. I was pushing myself so hard that I felt pressured to make my business succeed. I had put the pressure on myself; I wanted to prove to myself and my family. I needed and wanted to provide for us. I tried to be positive, stay motivated, and push through.

Unfortunately, I was mostly deluded. I went in on myself and stopped really communicating with my husband. I was embarrassed that I was getting inconsistent sales, which took longer than I had hoped to grow financially. I was networking, building connections, producing great design work and had happy clients. But the yo-yo-ing of incoming money made it hard to plan or relax. I couldn't take any design project for granted.

It wasn't until I opened my eyes to my situation, took responsibility and communicated with my husband that I could make real progress. Even as a solopreneur, I'm not alone, and using my support network is important.

2: Gratitude

We can get so wrapped up in finding something to be grateful for. We're trying to convince ourselves that it's really not so bad. That other person has it much worse than we do, so we shouldn't complain or worry.

I remember listening to 'The Secret' and the chapter all about the 'attitude of gratitude' and absolutely loved it at the time.

Now, I'm not saying that being grateful or practising gratitude is a harmful thing to do. I agree it is, for the most part, a positive and healthy thing to do.

However, it comes back to allowing you to take a moment (or however long you need) to process what is going on in your life. Really feel what you feel, whether it's sadness, anger or guilt. It's ok to feel those negative emotions. It's part of our human experience.

Once you've sat with those emotions for a bit... dust yourself off. Then count your blessings and be grateful. Don't sweat it if you can't find something to be grateful for beyond breathing in and out or something seemingly small and insignificant. Don't force yourself to be in that 'attitude of gratitude'.

Back to the lemons, what actually works when you get handed a few?

Here are a few things that I have found have kept me going when the going gets tough:

- My vision for the future that I'm building towards.

- The mini-mission to move forward and make progress and action (however small).

- Recognising how far I've come so far and celebrating the wins and successes.

Vision

Having a vision for your life or business can be a bit airy fairy for some, or writing a vision statement is something only big corporations do. I have dabbled in creating my own vision. I have a vision board I put together in Canva and set it as my desktop picture on my laptop. I also have a physical one with cut-out pictures from magazines and printouts pinned on a corkboard by my desk.

In the last couple of years, I've really started to connect with my vision on a deeper level. It's taken some introspection and reflection to truly feel worthy and deserving of my dreams and goals. And on a practical level, my goals are achievable because I've been putting in the groundwork.

All that time I've been beavering away on my business, trying different ways to work with my clients and evolving has not been wasted. Yes, I've made mistakes, taken longer than planned, and shelved ideas for later. Now I realise I've been building the foundations.

I love those stories of wildly successful people. Think about Denise Duffield-Thomas and the number of lives she's helped. She's made millions, has a thriving business, and seems everywhere. Her success did not happen overnight. She started her coaching business in 2010, and not everything she put out there worked. Not everyone loves her. If she'd given up after a couple of years, she would not be making the impact she is today. I'm sure we wouldn't even know who she is.

My vision is personal to me. I've discovered that 6-figure this or 7-figure that does not fire me up. Yes, I want to earn money. Yes, I can earn more than I thought possible when studying at university and what I could earn as an employed creative at the top level.

My vision is to build a life and business that is meaningful to me and creatively fulfilling. And I want to have a positive impact on those around me.

Mission

I mentioned a mini mission because mission statements, like vision statements, can be vague. A mini mission could be boiled down to your priority project and linked to the actionable tasks on your to-do list. A mini-mission is more meaningful. It's about taking an aspect of your business or life and making it your top focus so you can progress and move it forward.

At the end of 2023, I launched my own mobile app. It's been on my list for 18 months and bounced up and down the list of importance. I would pick it up, work on it for a bit, and then get busy with client work or lose the motivation to work on it.

It took a bout of burnout in January 2023 for me to be reminded that I can have some good financial months when saying yes to every design project that comes along. The downsides are there are only so many hours in the day, and I need unlimited creative energy, which means a cap on my business growth and no room for flexibility if there's an emergency.

I'm a bit stubborn, so it took more reminders and lessons from my body and the universe to get me thinking. And then eventually taking the action.

The mobile app, called 'Build your brand with Canva', will be a pivotal part of my business in the future. It's the new home where I can put my Lovely Canva Club membership, which I've been running since 2020. And it's a great marketing tool to stick my lead magnet on.

To me, it's all of those businessy sales things. But more importantly, it means that I prioritise my time and energy. It's an important part of my vision and mission as it's the tool I can use to help people and create that impact I mentioned. It also represents time leverage and a stable income as my courses and membership on the app grow.

It's not just a snazzy app. It is one of the vehicles that help me have a balanced business that makes me happy.

Celebrating

My final practical method when things are tough or you need to pick me up is to recognise how far you've come.

I've fallen into the trap of thinking that you need to earn loads of money to be successful. It blinded me to the achievements and successes that I already had.

Take a moment to step back and think about your past year. Have a look at the camera roll on your phone to give you a prompt. What were your highlights?

At the end of 2022, I gave myself the challenge to apply for several awards as a way to grow my visibility. It was a huge step out of my comfort zone. I'm not someone who naturally shouts about how good I am and had to learn how to stop hiding under a rock!

I first put myself forward for the f: Entrepreneur Top 100 list and was delighted to make the 2023 list. That gave me the confidence to put myself forward for the international Indigo Design Awards and won the bronze in my category. I nominated myself for the Digital Women Awards and came runner-up in the digital freelancer category. And I'm most proud of winning the silver award in the creative category for the Best Business Women Awards. That one was a very involved application process, and I'd previously applied and not made it as a finalist. There were a couple of awards that I applied for that didn't make the cut.

I'm proud of those awards and glad I put myself forward. An award or two does not make me want to high-five myself or walk around with a swagger. But when I'm having a bit of self-doubt, I can glance at my awards and stamp that negative thought out before it ruins my day or holds me back.

Celebrate your milestones, achievements and all the wins. You deserve it!

Now, back to the words' joy' and 'flow' I mentioned at the beginning.

Joy for me is in the small things. It's a version of happiness that's more attainable. It's going for a walk on a crisp sunny day in winter. It's that first taste of an indulgent chocolate pudding or snuggles and cuddles on the sofa. A big source of joy for me is creating. I love designing for my clients, creating Canva templates, doodling and oil painting. It's just as well that being a designer is my day job!

Flow is about being in the moment. It's alignment. Being discerning in the choices I make. I'm releasing those self-imposed deadlines and pressures. Instead, I'm taking action step by step.

"It's not about being happy all the time or being sure of all your choices. It's about knowing that life is precious, even when it's tough." - **Topher Kearby** -

MARLENE NEUMANN

2024

CHAPTER 11

Finding the Needle in a Haystack

by Marlene Neumann

As I sat staring out of my office window, listening to the loud echoing call of South Africa's Hadedah bird, my head was twirling, and my heart was racing. I could feel my mind trying to find answers. Deep inside me, I knew that my life had to change, but the news I had just received was not what I expected change to look like.

Was I truly about to die? Was my life over at the age of 38? I felt the blood drain from my head and flood my body. I was stunned. A deep, calming voice inside me said, 'Let go'. I had this sinking feeling. Stuck in mental anguish, a prison of thick walls surrounded my mind as I tried to figure a way out of this deep, lonely pit I found myself in.

I had always seen myself as vivacious, outgoing, driven and ambitious. I was 38 years old, at the top of my game, and a leader in my field as a fine art photographer and head of department at a leading art school in South Africa. What more could I want? My life ticked all the boxes. I had everything I thought success looked like.

The world I had created collapsed in front of my eyes when the doctor told me I had three months left to live. They had found a lump in my left breast, and it looked like it was going to kill me.

I felt immense fear and turmoil. I'd hit a brick wall and could not escape myself anymore. Life as I knew it began to crumble. Something as huge as this had to threaten me in order for me to take my life seriously. The domino effect began - I left a 7-year relationship, stopped meeting my circle of friends, and transformed my diet. My whole perception of the world changed.

I felt incredibly fragile, alone and unlovable. The worst part was that what threatened me was invisible. I remember sitting night after night bargaining with God to give me a second chance. Pleading, praying for direction, guidance, a sign.

It wasn't until the day I was sitting in the waiting room of the x-ray department clutching a book someone had given me called *The Power of Now* by Eckhart Tolle that I allowed myself to hear God's answer. 'Now' had always felt like a nightmare to me, the planner, the striver, the achiever.

Something shifted in me that day. I felt a release of the pressure I had been holding onto. 'Surrender and let go, Marlene, it's out of your control'. My mind eventually began to move into the background as I taught myself to calm down, bringing stillness to my body and allowing my mind to quieten, creating space for the fear inside to dissolve into the power of presence.

If doctors ask me what cured me, I tell them it was that moment I let go of my suffering and surrendered to living in the present moment.

I realised I wanted to live my life fully - now. Fear was in the future in the construct of my mind. Courage stepped up when I created space around my thinking.

For the next few months, I tried to find my balance. Was that easy? No! It was terrifying watching every foundation I'd built my world upon collapse. People kept giving me advice, telling me what to do. Sometimes, I felt like I was sitting in the middle of a 7-lane highway, trying to find peace and quiet but unable to listen to my heart.

Looking back at that brave girl sitting in the waiting room, I see her courage and desperation. She decided to change her world. She stopped clinging to people around her like lifebelts, believing they could help her navigate the nightmare.

Nothing was certain. The life I had was over. My Soul had pushed the pause button and wanted me to change direction.

The cancer was never going to kill me, but the fear of the future - that was terrifying. I had to bring myself into alignment physically, mentally, spiritually, and emotionally. The whole of me had to heal, not just the physical. I chose the most difficult path. I chose the natural path of learning to understand myself better. I am a beautiful human being filled with spirit and love, and I had to get to know the whole of me.

After three months of churning confusion, going back and forth between my heart and head, I finally made the most difficult decision ever. I chose to have my left breast removed or face certain death. I realised that the most powerful healer was that I had to love myself first. No one was going to do that for me. It was obvious in my heart when I made that decision. There was no turning back.

My world turned upside down and inside out. I had lost my job, friends, and my entire life of who I thought I was. I hardly recognised myself. I have felt like Alice in Wonderland for most of my life, not knowing what or how to be in this life. Being in the present moment introduced me to a lifelong journey of healthy eating, thinking consciously and deep meditation. My spiritual quest had begun.

I was pushed through a dark tunnel to the light. It took the dying of my old self to discover that success is a humbling experience where life happens only in the moment that we have right in front of us.

After the operation, because I had chosen myself, there was no self-loathing. I simply had a love for my divine feminine. From that moment on, I knew that my physical body did not define my inner world. My body and my identity didn't define me.

There was something mystical calling me back home. I've journeyed through many painful memories, undergoing various mental and emotional releases of childhood trauma that my body has held onto. It sounds so simple, but it is a huge challenge when we have had a life training the mind to think and plan what lies in the future.

The depth of who we are is the most under-taught phenomenon. I have experienced a deep connection to Source, which made me realise that inner peace is not outside ourselves. Through meditation and hypnotherapy, I managed to save my life, realising that Life is only NOW.

Understanding this deep presence resides in each of us, I began teaching people inner peace through photography. I learnt to capture that split moment of stillness that Nature desperately tries to teach us. Our bodies are in a rhythm with Nature when we focus our attention on our breath, which is only ever now!

We have trained our minds to live in the future, but our lives are only ever now. When we practise this daily, we can heal ourselves from all sorts of ailments. Life is happening at this precise moment you are reading this. Through simple processes, I teach my students to still their minds and allow life to flow through them as they tune into Nature. At first, this appears strange, but as we live our lives from this new awareness, the present moment is the only way to live - a new, more natural way of being human.

Learning to regulate my thoughts and my breath, I know that life happens in the present moment. I know this sounds easy to do, but the mind and ego constantly want us to follow a different course. It takes discipline to rise above the mind and bring awareness to the here and now. I can calm my body down and feel this eternal peace at any moment I choose.

We have not been taught to become aware of creating space around our thoughts and feelings. This process saved my life and put me in a whole new direction, uncovering layers of how to be human. The present moment is where Nature and animals commune with Source. My life-threatening illness was my grace period. It allowed me to access a part of myself I never knew existed.

I have accomplished many material things in this life, but none of them are so great as to experience living fully in this moment, to become one with my breath and with all life. My anxiety and stress levels have very little effect on me when I choose how to react to a thought or feeling. In a world that promotes chaos, I encourage and teach this process of stillness and centering ourselves, aligning mind-body-spirit, where I feel grounded and connected to Mother Earth.

Being able to drop straight into that place of bliss within each of us is like finding a needle in the haystack. It is a gift to be able to share this with others. I sometimes find that when I am totally still inside like the clear water in a glass, others around experience inner stillness too. To be able to use this hidden secret of being human is my greatest success. It saved my life.

“

Strong women aren't born,
they're forged in the fires
they've had to walk through.
They're warriors with hearts of
gold!

SILVER RAVENWOLF

NAOMI RICHES MBE PLY DL

2024

CHAPTER 12

From Playground to Podium

By Naomi Riches MBE PLY DL

I am sure you are all very familiar with the voice in your head that stops you in your tracks, that holds you back, that doubts you? More often than not, it is significantly louder than the optimistic, confident and gutsy voice in your head. But who does that voice belong to?

When I was invited to be part of this book, it didn't take long for me to jump in with both feet. Yes, definitely, WOW, I would love to. There was however, a part my mind trying to hold me back, after all, what have I got to say that people have not already heard from someone else?

Then I realised, the doubting voice, the part of my mind that sabotages me, is precisely why I should put pen to paper, or rather fingers to keys and get typing.

When I stood on the medal podium at the London 2012 Paralympic Games, and the gold medal was placed around my neck, surreal but tangible and very shiny; I could feel the roar of the crowd in my core… I knew in that crowd I had friends and family who were feeling the joy, the pride, elation… and if I am honest, the relief with me.

In that otherworldly moment, a memory tip toed through my mind of an old teacher of mine who was overheard talking to a colleague, saying something like, *"that's the blind girl from my class… unfortunately we have to have girls like that at our school".*

I didn't dwell on it at the time, the moment was too special; but that memory is a harsh reminder of the many people, when I was younger, that never even tried to see beyond my disability, but who did try to define me by what they perceived as my limitation, my 'problem'.

Yes, being a Paralympian automatically defines you as being disabled; but I believe it is your abilities that define what you achieve in your sport, not your disability.

I was born with a visual impairment called Achromatopsia, which means that I have no colour vision, I struggle with bright light and quickly changing light conditions; and my visual acuity is poor. One eye condition really isn't enough though… I also have Nystagmus, so my eyes are continually moving to try and focus, and I can't judge the speed of moving objects. My eyes also work separately, I have monocular vision, so judging depth and space is compromised. It is quite a cocktail and that combination means that I am Registered Blind.

From a very early age, things were challenging, every day activities had to be thought through, they were not impossible to achieve, they just had to be done differently.

I had very little support at school and was a sitting target for the bullies; quite literally in PE, especially tennis and rounders which were hell on earth. There was a small handful of teachers who were incredible, doing their absolute best to make lessons achievable for me but I'm sorry to say that they were in the minority. I felt unimportant. I always got the impression that as far as the school was concerned, as long as the other twenty-nine children in the class were doing well, that was enough.

I left school on the back foot, with little to no self-confidence, with indifferent grades and truly feeling that I had very little to offer the world. What on earth would I do when I left education?

Beyond the school walls, Mum and Dad did everything they could to help me to find myself, supported my passions and encouraged my talents. I was not the kind of child that would sit still for long; I would fill my time, after the completion of HOURS of homework with swimming, trampolining, self-defence, archery and any outward-bound activity I could get involved in… but my favourite place in the world to be was in the spare room, losing myself in a talking book and filling up forests of sketch pads; painting or drawing whatever was in, or perhaps on my mind.

Oh, and that was another thing about school… children can be incredibly cruel when they don't understand. I'm blind remember, how come I am so good at art? I had no idea, I just was, I was creative with a huge imagination, escapism maybe?

After fighting with the local education authority for funding, I went to RNIB New College in Worcester for my A-Levels; a small school in Worcester that had one hundred and twelve students from year seven through to year thirteen. Being in that environment, I felt I belonged… it was the start of me realising that there was so much more to me than my eye condition. When you are in a school with other blind and partially sighted people, who often have additional disabilities added into the mix, you soon come to understand that it is not your disability that everyone is putting front and centre of your existence, that is only one facet of you, you are so much more.

As I have already mentioned, I was an active, energetic person who had to have something to go and do; to be fair, that hasn't changed in the slightest. There was a great variety of things to get involved with at Worcester College, to broaden the interests and horizons of the students… and it was at Worcester that I discovered the intense, tough but oh so rewarding sport of rowing.

Midland Television got in touch with the college one day to ask if we had any young people who wanted to be on the news in a piece about young disabled people being active in sport, but it was far more specific than that… it was a call for four students, who hopefully had an interest in rowing, to go to Henley-on-Thames, to Leander Rowing Club. We were to row with Steve Redgrave and Matthew Pinsent, now Sir Steve and Sir Matthew, Ed Coode and Tim Foster.

They were sporting GIANTS, not just in achievement but in height and power. Sitting in a boat behind Matthew Pinsent was, well, to be totally honest I can't quite remember, but I do remember him saying to be afterwards words to the effect of *'you're quite good'*. What me? A sporting legend has just told me I was *'quite good'*, I was speechless… he had seen past my disability and looked at me as a young person, a fellow rower, nothing more.

Wind forward a few years to April 2004, and I got a phone call from a man called Simon Goodey who was the then Coach of the British Adaptive (disabled) Rowing Team, to ask if I wanted to trial for the team. Due to a rule change from the International Governing Body, FISA, all crews had to be a mixed gender crew of two men and two women, the cox could either be male or female. Up to this point, the Great Britain Adaptive Coxed Four had consisted of four male rowers and a female cox and had already won the Gold medal at the World Rowing Championships in Milan, Italy. The bar was set very very high… but missing an opportunity like this would be insane!!!

In rowing, a coxed four is four rowers with one oar each and a coxswain, or cox who is usually about 50-55kg in weight. The Cox steers the boat, delivers calls to the boat to make sure you are all doing the same thing at the same time in terms of technical changes, and changes in speed. In races, they are also responsible to seeing what is happening in the rest of the field and getting their crew to respond together if and when necessary.

So, how did Simon get my number, and why on earth did he think I was the right fit for the team? The older we get, the more we understand it is truly who you know not what you know that matters; a friend from Worcester College was in the 2003 Gold medal winning crew and had passed my number over. The three criteria that Simon needed to fill a seat in the boat were very simple, he was looking for a tall, disabled female… tick, tick and tick.

Talk about a steep learning curve… four months later, when looking back, after what appears to be only a handful of outings together, we were kitted out with our GB Rowing Lycra's and heading to Banyoles, Spain. In the foothills of the Pyrenees mountains, Lake Banyoles is just over two kilometres long and is where the Oympic Rowing Regatta was held for the Barcelona Games in 1992. It was a stunning location for my first international rowing event… but unsurprisingly, it was also slightly intimidating! On August 1st 2004, we lined up for my first World Rowing Championships FINAL, I was convinced my heartbeat could be heard by the supporters in the stands and all I could really think was 'what the…'

Three minutes and thirty-nine seconds later we were World Champions.

Crossing that line first wasn't really about becoming World Champion for me, strange as that might sound. I knew how important sporting World Championships were, and what they meant to the athletes and supporters, but having not been a follower of sport, it was not the idea of the title that tempted me into the boat. It was more the chance to see if I could do it, if it was a way to defy others perceptions of my ability in a very public way. This is all in hindsight of course, at the time it was smiles all round and singing Spandau Ballet's GOLD down the phone to our families as we called up each in turn; and I went home with some pretty awesome GB kit.

There is not enough time or space here for me to take you through the challenging but exciting, sometimes soul destroying, often character building, remarkable and magnificent decade in the GB Rowing Squad… perhaps that is for another book.

So back to where we started, the 2nd of September, at the London 2012 Paralympic Games, at Eton Dorney.

Sitting on that start line, I was not thinking 'what the…' as I had done in in Spain eight years before. I had sat on countless start lines since then and though I was no less nervous, I had learnt to have a little control over my thought process, ditching what was unhelpful and focusing on the things I could control. We had one job… just get to the finish line before anyone else! All I was focusing on was what our Cox, Lily van den Broeke, lying down in the bow of the boat, was telling us to do to keep the boat straight in the characteristic Eton Dorney Cross wind. I was also visualising the start sequence that we had practised until it became muscle memory, it was just thirteen strokes to get our Coxed Four up to full speed, then move to the next phase.

Pam Relph was sat behind me, David Smith in front of me and James Roe was in the Stroke Seat… his job was to set that relentless punchy rhythm we knew so well. We were in lane three and the Germans, who had quite spectacularly won their heat, were in lane four.

The German crew were fast out of the blocks and held us off through half way, through 400 meters to go, through 300 meters to go I think… I am not sure as I could hear nothing but that Dorney Roar, making the water fizz, and drowning out all that Lily was telling us and the sounds of the German crew. I didn't even hear the finish line buzzer, all I knew was that David had collapsed back into my lap and the volume of the crowd somehow became even louder. I turned to Pam, unsure of what had happened in the closing stages of the race, and… above the roar… I heard, *'WE WON GOLD NAOMI, WE WON!!!'.*

This time, unlike 2004, the win was all about becoming Paralympic Champions… well almost all. For me, there was still a small part that was hoping all those who had not expected me to achieve, who had not seen my potential, who had even gone so far as to say so, were watching the TV.

Rest assured, just because I mastered that negative, nasty voice in my head for much of the time when I was an athlete, doesn't mean it has gone. It is still there, chipping away. I do have to keep reminding myself who that voice really belongs to and where it originated from.

Passing this message on, sharing my lived experiences, and helping others realise and even fulfil their potential is now what drives me and what I have based my business around. There is no greater privilege for me than speaking to a client during or after working with them and hearing what they have learned, what they have achieved or what perception they have blown out of the water.

We all have limitations of one kind or another, barriers to overcome, mental ditches to jump… and many of them, you will have placed there for yourself over time. I have learned that more often than not they begin in your past with another person's view, perception or misunderstanding… or just because they wanted to be cruel. That voice in your head really belongs to them, not you, but is has morphed over time, becoming a voice you think is yours. It is so ingrained, you believe what it is telling you.

Just remember, there are very few people in your life who really and truly understand what you are capable of… you might not yet realise it yourself… but don't let anyone limit your potential with their perception of what you can achieve. Leave that with them, don't let it linger as a voice in your head.

"

You are braver than you believe,
stronger that you seem, and
smarter than you think.

A.A. MILNE

REBECCA LEEK SMITH

2024

CHAPTER 13

24 hours to leave

By Rebecca Leek Smith

Leave your home, children, cat, dog, friends, and family. You cannot tell a soul. Wait what? How can I just up and leave? Where do I go? The feeling of fear and uncertainty made my body shake, I instantly felt ice cold, and my mouth dried up completely. I had gone into shock.

I had been trying to leave my extremely abusive husband of 17 years for over a year; we had five children together, three living with me and two with him. How dare I try and leave him? As far as he was concerned, I belonged to him, end of story.

I thought by leaving him that, the abuse would stop, but it did not. It continued. He would not stop, the constant telephone calling, turning up everywhere I went, using the children, making verbal threats, smashing the doors of the house, petrol poured on my car, using his vehicle to ram me in my car, his constant suicide threats... It was relentless. I was living in a continual state of fear and anxiety; feelings of dread engulfed me. I could not eat or sleep and had a physical pain in my stomach that made me vomit. I had lost so much weight that I dropped a shoe size and at 5ft 2 inches, I was a tiny six stone. He was 6'7' and 18 stone, and his presence terrified me, especially knowing exactly what he could do.

I knew in my heart that I would eventually end up dead. Either by him killing me or by taking my own life from this horrendous torture and his malicious manipulation of the children, I felt so low; how would this end?

I was desperate; I needed support. Talking to the Police was a huge no.

In his family, you were never conditioned to speak to the old bill or any outside professional; these people cannot be trusted. What if they tell social services and they take my children away? Or what if they believed my husband, who was trying to convince people that I had had a nervous breakdown because I was attempting to split his family up? Seriously, how will I get help if I do not tell people what is happening? I was so scared and had no confidence in my own ability.

Eventually, I spoke to a local domestic abuse support group, which put me in touch with the National Centre for Domestic Violence to gain a non-molestation order for protection. I did it. I told people what was happening, and they wanted to help and support me. It felt good, but it felt wrong going behind his back; petrified, I thought he would go absolutely mental.

I was granted the non-molestation order by the Family Court (eventually, it was granted for 13 years, one of the longest in UK history). Still, he took no notice of it whatsoever. I found the courage to call the Police as much as possible, but he believed he was above the law. Over 12 months into the order, he breached it daily, was charged 26 times, arrested, and released repeatedly.

Then, the Police received confidential intelligence that he was trying to purchase a firearm. His constant harassment towards me and the well-documented statistic that women are at the most risk of death when they attempt to leave a perpetrator, they had to get me out within 24 hours.

Arriving at a women's refuge, I genuinely believed the staff would make me return; I was conditioned to think he could control everyone. They promised I could stay and would not send me back. I felt so lucky to be there. Still scared, but I was safe. That was seven years ago.

The years of abuse on every level and the trauma had taken its toll on me, and I was diagnosed with CPTSD. I had family court cases upon court cases to deal with, as well as criminal proceedings against him for stalking with fear of violence. Living in a refuge and technically homeless, three children with me and two that I could not communicate appropriately with, life was extremely difficult, I did not know who I was.

Apart from my children, the one aspect of my life that brought me joy was creating. Art and creativity were my passion.

Through all the crap I was dealing with, I was encouraged to do what I wanted regarding my creativity. It allowed me to put my mind into something I loved (I covered the refuge in my creations!). Building myself up, trying to let go of all the opposing ideologies he had made me believe about myself, I battled so hard to gain self-esteem and confidence. But slowly, I did it. I have always been very appreciative, so I practised gratitude daily. I started talking a lot. All the years I had been made to be quiet were behind me now, and you could not shut me up!

I chatted with a lovely lady who could see how passionate I was about my creativity. As the head of the art school at Wolverhampton, she invited me to start a university degree in foundation arts. I had no portfolio because I had to leave everything behind and was still in refuge, but she made it happen. I felt like I was the luckiest woman alive!

In 2019, I started Foundation Art. I then went on to do my degree in textiles and surface patterns. Having my degree to do, alongside all the stresses, was unbelievably difficult. Some days, I was so detached due to anxiety that I could not physically move. Some weeks, my greatest achievement was just having a shower. I still looked over my shoulder every day. But I did it. I stopped to rest but kept going. At this time, I moved into my new home and had my terminally ill mother live with me so I could care for her. She sadly passed away in 2021. Court cases were still raging, I was supporting my brother through a mental breakdown, and my heart was breaking for my other children, and I could not help no matter how hard I tried. I was still trying to be a good mother to the children in my care and help them understand the situation. "You have to go through it to get through it" was my mantra. I needed to be a positive role model, let my children see me succeed, and finally have a career in art.

I had many achievements throughout my time at university and graduated with first and two awards. One of the awards was the Wolverhampton University Chancellor's Award for Initiative and Resilience in Extreme Circumstances! I was so proud of myself and shocked that I had achieved so high! I finally found who I was.

The day after my graduation, the seven years of family court cases finally concluded!

Don’t let fear hold you back, you deserve to be happy.

REBECCA RYAN

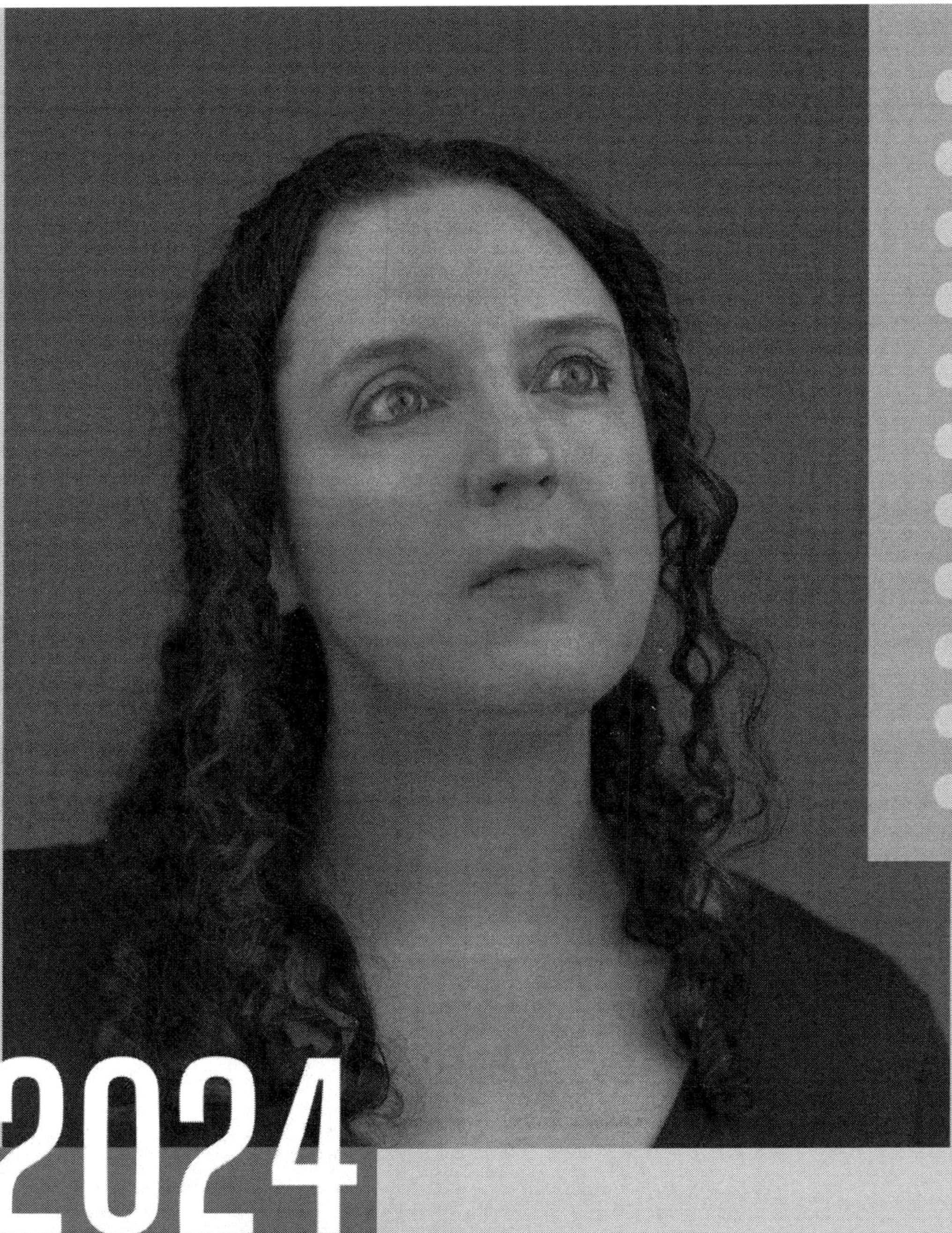

2024

CHAPTER 14

Finding Calm in the Chaos

By Rebecca Ryan

My mum died suddenly from Cancer when I was 22, and my world came crashing down. What followed was a year of burying the pain and a year of pure escapism. I moved from the small Welsh town where I had grown up to West London, where the doors opened to a veritable palace of drugs and denial. But the chaos in my mind remained.

Music has always been a place of solace for me. Moments of calm in the storm. Growing up in an abusive household, I escaped into the world of musical theatre from the age of ten. My mum loved me dearly, but the dynamics between her and my stepdad made for a tempestuous home. He was incredibly jealous of how much she loved me, leading to constant conflict. The theatre provided me with some security and a new family to be a part of, but it didn't fill the void. My stepfather was distant, disparaging and dismissive. At thirteen years old, the church seemed to offer the father figures I had longed for in the vicars and youth leaders and it did for several years. Music continued to be a key refuge and provided me with some equilibrium and happiness.

To rewind a little, I had not had the most positive start with male role models. My biological father did not want to know me. I found out why after my mum died, which explained an awful lot. She had a very difficult time, with spells in a mental hospital in the late 60s. Her first husband was a Russian lecturer at the university. He was impotent and paid a doctor to tell Kay (my mum) that she was infertile. They adopted a baby, who, it transpired, had brain damage, resulting in her being taken away and placed in an institution.

This was a significant factor in my mum's nervous breakdown, coupled with the ending of her marriage. While she was under section, her husband moved a lover, another student, into the home and placed Mum's belongings in bin bags.

After Mum was discharged from the hospital in Carmarthen, she moved to London and set up Kay's Bureau, a marriage agency. She had become pregnant and miscarried by a transient lover and set up the agency with the express purpose of finding a sperm donor, as she was desperate to have a baby. She met my biological father, a journalist from London (who I apparently get my curly hair from). She timed their encounters with her fertility cycle. When she announced she was pregnant, he was outraged (I have a copy of the letter he wrote her) and he cut ties. Nine months later, I was born, and she controversially claimed child support (much to my grandparents' dismay) until she met my stepdad eighteen months later.

It was a marriage of convenience. He had lost his first wife to suicide the previous year and had a ten-year-old daughter. I was eighteen months. He was damaged. But providing a home for both children seemed a mutually beneficial solution. I think he did care about Mum in his own way. But my earliest childhood memory is one of violence. Financially, it was a secure home but emotionally a disaster.

The sexual abuse I was subjected to by my neighbour when I was six affected me more than I realised at the time. I kept it a secret until I was sixteen, partly due to guilt, partly denial and fear. When I spoke up, it was brushed under the carpet with moderate ease, and I was expected to forget about it and move on. I knew at this point I had a choice, to let it define me and be overcome with bitterness and anger or use it to make me stronger and more resilient.

It worked for a while but definitely impacted my romantic relationships moving forward. I married young but soon realised I sought security and safety rather than an intimate relationship. The wedding was difficult - my stepdad walked out after the ceremony, and the best man (who I had fortunately known since I was ten) had to give two speeches. I had never felt so rejected and never received an apology. But I was not completely surprised.

A year after my mum died, the black dog reared its head. A month after she passed, I started my first job as a Drama and English teacher at the secondary school she had worked at.

I was pretty resilient for a while and tried to throw myself into my career, but the darkness of grief crept in and began to envelop me. A year after my mum died, my stepfather visited me. During a conversation about the will, he told me that 'I was the most selfish, self-centred female he had ever met, and he would rather die than see me again.' At that moment, I decided it is healthier to cut some people out of your life for your well-being, no matter how much you hope a relationship will change. We haven't spoken in over twenty-five years. And I have made my peace with that.

At the time, though, my world and marriage was imploding. I chose to escape, running away to London and embarking on a year of avoiding the pain, indulging in a hedonistic lifestyle and heading towards self-destruction. A string of sexual encounters filled the void for a while, combined with forays into alcohol and drugs. Spending most of my childhood and early adulthood in a small Welsh town, splitting my time between the church and the theatre, I was not exposed to many nefarious influences. I became a little like a child in a sweet shop. London became the playground I needed to further numb the pain. A cocktail of substances and a doomed relationship with a coke addict enabled me to disappear into an abyss that, at the time, seemed far easier than dealing with my grief. 18 months of therapy later...

I met a wonderful man when I was 33. Fast forward four years, and we were married. It was the happiest day of my life, and we were content for a while. Then, the lies came to light. A year after our wedding, I discovered that Steve had two grown-up children he had not seen since they were toddlers. This should have rung alarm bells, but I stayed. The marriage commitment meant something (and I didn't want a second failed marriage before I was forty). Soon after this revelation, he lost his driving licence for six months after being caught speeding, and a year later, he lost a lucrative job at a brewery for drinking on the job. Both of these pretty significant events were kept from me for weeks.

And still, I stayed. But the distance grew, and the clouds became more oppressive. I knew there was a gaping hole in my life. I left my English and Drama teacher job in an outstanding secondary school to work for a mental health hospital.

I was disillusioned by constant government changes to the curriculum and the need to jump through endless data hoops. I wanted to make more of a difference.

Working with young people with severe mental health issues is still, to this day, the most challenging and rewarding job I have ever done. It was where I rediscovered my love of music and realised I deserved more than the loveless marriage I felt trapped in.

In September 2016, I ended my marriage. He did not fight it, which confirmed that my decision was wise. I threw myself into my music. I learnt to play the guitar and played as many open mics and showcases as possible. Music became, once more, a solace and source of healing. A year to the day after my marriage ended, my first original song poured out of me, and a new chapter began.

My chaos was calmed through the cathartic process of songwriting. The pain I had buried poured out in song. Six months later, I met my best friend. I strongly believe that people come into your life at a certain time for a reason.

Ash and I hit it off immediately. We met through a mutual friend, who asked me to do backing vocals on the album Ash was producing. Within a few weeks, I worked on lyrics and melodies for some of his unfinished ideas. We started writing songs together a few months later, and our duo Tu-kay & Ryan was born. We shared a common passion and drive to spread a little hope and positivity through our music. In 2018 and 2019, we released two EPs and started to receive local, national and international radio plays. We planned our debut album in 2020.

Then COVID hit. As gigging was impossible, we bubbled up and took to writing and live streaming. We were able to reach a whole new audience at a time when a glimmer of hope was much needed. Our friendship grew, and we became more like siblings. We released two more EPs in 2021 and 2022, Passage of Time and The Little Things. Moving forward, more of the songs we wrote became focused on the power of friendship and a new debut album was written. It seemed fitting that we should call it Companion.

I was revelling in my new musical life. It gave me a sense of fulfilment and self-worth that I had not felt before. Then, I started to feel off-kilter. I assumed it was a result of the various lockdowns. I was angry and irritable for no reason and incredibly emotional.

The rage I started to unleash on Ash was horrible for him and made me feel pretty bad about myself.

It took me over a year to realise, after conversations with female friends and some research of my own, that it might be the start of the perimenopause. I tried a variety of herbal remedies, reflexology and reiki. The latter two definitely helped. But then the anxiety hit. I started to feel so out of control, and my mood and emotions became totally unpredictable. I tolerated it for a couple of months, and then it began to find its way into my calm place - my music. I was lucky to have a menopause specialist nurse at my doctor's surgery and booked an appointment.

I'm sure it is different for every woman. The fear of being unable to do what I love most made me finally seek help. My journey with Tu-kay & Ryan so far has seen us win multiple awards and receive glowing reviews for our live performances and recordings. We released our debut album Companion in November 2023 to critical acclaim and have brought shimmers of light to a growing number of audiences through our optimistic lyrics and message of hope. We both genuinely believe there is always a glimmer of light in the darkness, no matter how far away it may seem. This has resonated with me incredibly since the perimenopause reared its head.

At the time of writing this, I have been on HRT for nearly eight weeks. It is still a rollercoaster at the moment, but I am hopeful that a combination of HRT, reiki, meditation and conversations with other women who have been or are going through the same thing will help me regain some equilibrium.

Until then, I am taking some time away from work - a wise person told me recently that you need to put the oxygen mask on yourself first before trying to help others. Music continues to be an essential part of my therapy. I never dreamed that when Ash and I started writing together, the lyrics we designed to help others would resonate with me so much. Despite the current struggles I am facing, I am excited about the future and the possibilities it holds.

'You can't change what's out of your control.

Learn to live your life before you're old.

There's so much story that remains untold.

If you keep on searching, you will find, if you give yourself a little time.'

RITA PRESTON
2024

CHAPTER 15

Rocking On

by Rita Preston

One year ago, I faced a dilemma: accept one more volunteer position when I felt stretched in too many directions already or allow my refusal to accept the position (knowing that if replacement officers were not found, the organisation would be required to fold) to kill an amazing community organisation (our local fair). No pressure.... We were short on volunteers and had an immediate need.

I was nominated to be secretary to finish the remaining half of a two-year term that had been vacated. Catching my breath and eyes welling with tears, my voice cracked. Attempting to explain the family worries that we'd kept private out of respect for those going through stressful moments, my sorrow spilt forth. There were a few gasps in the room as I emphasised that my primary focus was helping specific family members. I had commitments to other organisations as well.

Without hesitation, a motion was made to create an assistant secretary position to help me. I told them I would give them one year. We filled the vacant positions, and the organisation could advance into 2023. As we departed the meeting, several kind individuals approached me separately, letting me know that each would be there if I needed a hand. All I had to do was say the word, and they would be there.

Teamwork!

I am not given to tears in meetings. I might cry in the shower or in the rain, but as a rule, I quit crying in front of people ten years ago after our daughter and newborn granddaughter passed away. It wasn't a conscious decision.

I was raised to keep emotions in check publicly, keep a stiff upper lip, and put out the proper good public image.

Anyway, the thought of dripping tears during any type of professional meeting is entirely out of the question.

But, I shed tears. There were empathetic looks. I was not alone.

I thought to myself, "What have I done?" I drove home and shared the 'exciting' news with my husband.

We were also awaiting word on his back and hip pain, which had become excruciating. We feared he was due for more surgery (as a reprise to surgery 26+ years prior). Knowing it would not be a rapid recovery, much weighed on our hearts. My dear husband wished me 'good luck' on my new 'job'.

He knew. I knew.

Neither of us is prone to shy away from community needs. We overextend, no matter how much we must leave undone at home. We help others. There is no concrete reason for why or how; we just try to help where we can when asked.

Our new board moved into 2023, and our roles were being filled.

Prior year paperwork and research into who should be doing what ensued. The former officers had left lists of what had been included in their tasks.

That was a huge asset.

Hubby ended up with hip surgery instead of spinal surgery by January. As winter progressed, we both fell victim to covid.

Another organisation where I serve as the public relations officer suddenly needed a secretary. I agreed to be appointed for the time being.

Suddenly, spring was at hand, and I realised that I needed to book bands for the upcoming summer fair in August. Six (6) nights of entertainment! Somehow, my brain hadn't registered that bands fell to me. Yikes!

I've been blessed with many experiences in various organisations, from veterans' posts to parades to Sunday and Bible schools.

I've worked in secretarial capacities, as a director of programs, treasurer, and a few others over the years.

Booking bands for concert situations? Nope, not in my repertoire.

How hard could this be? Looking through past records, I discovered that many of our past entertainers had conflicts, disbanded, or were not going to work out for us for 2023 for many reasons.

Racking my brain, with solid support from my assistant, our treasurer, and our board members (whom I'm honoured to call friends), I put out feelers. One by one, nights were scheduled. Some entertainers came from further locations than most of our 'locals' and sent their contracts to my fair for my review and signature. More complex than our organisation traditionally offered, I reviewed their formats, made notes, signed theirs, and forwarded our own version for their signature. Some were content with our version of the paperwork. Double paperwork, perhaps, but bases covered the first time for me.

Learning on the fly. (This is not the first time, nor will it be the last!)

Prices were higher than what we traditionally budgeted.

Negotiating, pleading our cause for lower fees, and praying.

Overbudget. I felt defeated early on and in a panic.

I had only five out of six nights scheduled when our publication was sent to the print shop.

I had failed.

The published schedule was incomplete. Saturday night simply listed a “Special Saturday Surprise”.

Oh, how I hoped we had a great surprise!

Sweating. Nervous.

Family obligations. And that additional appointed secretarial position in the other organisation. (Had I refused the appointment, that organisation would have also been forced to fold due to the by-laws.)

Walking tightropes. On the edge all summer long.

Falling into engagement with a couple of musical groups who cut us amazing deals helped my stress level. However, I still felt behind the 8-ball for every task throughout the summer.

On a whim and with a prayer, I reached out to an award-winning Nashville recording artist hailing from a nearby state. I had met her several years prior at a convention and was impressed with her genuinely kind demeanour.

We emailed back and forth, and I committed to signing her, praying there would be a way to finance her visit.

Forget the tightrope; I was at the end of the limb!

I sent out specific sponsorship requests. I was dumbfounded when the response was returned! We had enough to cover our Saturday Night Closing Act!

We had coverage for a considerable portion of the week!

We would be under the budget of what the fair normally pays out of its meagre coffers.

I felt blessed and relieved!

I pushed a complete blitz on social media and our local media outlets, including newspapers, radio stations, and television stations.

I ran into one of the local radio disc jockeys about a week before the fair. He informed me that my organisation had better prepare to be overwhelmed due to our fantastic publicity. I thanked him for his kind support, started to move along, and he stopped me. His exact words escape me, but the context is: "You have no idea what you folks have done this summer. You're going to be amazed!"

I shared his words with a couple of our volunteers. We grinned, knowing that the weather could greatly affect our attendance. We heard that several non-profit vendors that normally attended were going to run shorter hours due to lacking enough able-bodied volunteers themselves. If not all the vendors were open, crowds might be smaller, hurting everyone's income potential.

There is a pandemic in the United States that has not come about from a virus: we suffer from a lack of volunteerism, seemingly made worse by the COVID-19 pandemic.

No one wants to work anymore.

That is a separate story.

So many factors affect a festival beyond the size of the grounds, the bank account, and the quantity of volunteers. Our fair includes livestock exhibits, homemaking exhibits, crafters, game vendors, non-profit food and game booths, and many weekly activities. Ours is one of the few left in our commonwealth with no fence, gates, or admission fee.

Monday night was opening entertainment night. It rained. A LOT. People took shelter under tiny porch roofs and stayed. By closing at 10pm, less than twenty people remained for our entertainers. But those few waited to get autographs and buy merchandise from our performers.

They asked us to bring the duo back in 2024! Our country / honky tonk duo was a hit!

Tuesday, the weather was gorgeous. Our next duo arrived full of life. People congregated and danced around the stage and bleachers throughout their performance, more than I have witnessed in my almost sixty years of life.

This duo of brothers played a mix of popular rock and pop, their original works spreading positivity. We rocked on Tuesday night!

Wednesday is parade night (which is held midweek to draw crowds to the fair when foot traffic might be slower). It was a picture-perfect night. I remain in awe of the talented folks of all ages who toot their horns, strut their stuff, twirl their batons, ride their beautiful horses, create amazing floats, and proudly carry flags. It's almost always HOT on parade night.

The parade is my 'baby', if you will. My late mum-in-law was involved and 'invited' me into the fold 30+ years ago.

It gets harder each year to visit the fairgrounds after the parade, but I wanted to ensure I saw our band, even briefly. My phone's battery was depleted. My assistant secretary was prepared and shot video for me.

Teamwork!

I didn't see much of the Wednesday night performer and his band, but he was well-received – a former hometown boy making it big in Pittsburgh.

Again, the listeners overflowed the bleachers and filled the areas around them!

Finally, feeling dead on my feet, I drove one of our granddaughters home (about 45 minutes away) before collapsing into my own bed a couple of hours later. (I was exhausted, but fostering her willingness to help and her new love of photography made my heart full.)

Each morning during the fair week, the alarm seemed more annoying and rang earlier and earlier. It wasn't, but it surely felt it.

Thursday night, I was able to enjoy our solo performance. He is a one-man show and very interactive with the crowd. Patriotic and popular music. Good weather. Another hit!

Picture taking! I try to glean photographs from others and take my own to be utilised on our website, social media, and in our digital scrapbook for the annual state convention.

Add that in here and there throughout the week!

I was thrilled to see our Baby Boomers congregating on the grounds awaiting our 50s-60s Do-Wopp style group on Friday night! They rocked Friday out of the park.

One day left, and my body felt it. Did I mention I have chronic pain, along with flare-ups in my left hip (due to a break and repair five years ago)? I danced (A LOT) on Tuesday night, and family members cautioned me I would need my cane again, maybe the walker. I danced anyway. I danced some every night.

I was committed to savouring the moment, feeling the music, and encouraging the crowds to enjoy the music by listening and interacting with the festival atmosphere.

I tried staying each night until the entertainers packed up and, on their way, home or close to it.

Our treasurer, one of my dearest friends, was my rock through the week. Every night, she reminded me to go home and get some rest. (She was there countless hours with our other volunteers all week, from trash pickup at dawn to running events in the animal arena.)

Teamwork!

I hadn't procured a camper for our entertainers to use as a green room. Only one had requested a green room specifically, a new request for our fair.

I had been too far behind when I started trying to book the camper. I had hyper-focused on getting the entertainers but not on the other amenities.

The local camper company indicated they'd love to work with us in 2024 with earlier notice.

Lesson learned.

Thankful for big sisters! My sister donated the use of her motorhome for the entire week, making sure it was in top form every day for the next crew of performers to use before and after their stage time, as well as during breaks.

I felt blessed.

Saturday, we faced a stormy forecast with possible tornadic activity. Our closing star posted her own live videos to social media to boost morale in the community, assuring us all that she had performed in the rain and had a good time.

She promised a good Nashville-style show!

Teamwork!

When our "Rockstar" arrived for sound-check, she verbally changed the formal contract so we wouldn't lose our crowd: she would start a bit late and play straight through to closing without any breaks! She is a good person, a stellar performer, and benevolent, not just an award winner!

The skies cleared, our volunteers weathered rumours the fair had shut down (um, NO!), and we rocked the night away to glorious music from modern rock style to that of old-fashioned country music legends.

Yes, I danced, even on the top tier of the bleachers! I danced with perfect strangers! (Granted, we don't have giant bleachers, but they are several tiers high.)

As I write this, Christmas Day is past, and 2024 is less than a week away. What will 2024 bring for these organisations, me, and my family?

In what I describe as a moment of weakness, I accepted a nomination for a 2-year term as the fair secretary and was elected in November.

Negotiations have begun, sponsorship letters were posted before Christmas, and I'm preparing for the parade. Our parade theme was picked at our November fundraiser, so we're ahead of the game as well.

As for the appointed extra position from earlier in the year, I declined the nomination, only to have that group write me in for a full 1-year term! Heavens!

I was requested not to decline after the election and to consider it until installation in January. Will I accept installation? Time will tell. I shall not answer in this chapter; let us await the sequel.

Planning, pre-planning, praying, patience, and plentiful friends and family have been key to this year's events. Pre-planning was lacking in accepting these extra positions.

I've always been a planner, a list-maker. I want to know what's coming and be prepared. (Maybe that's the part of my Girl Scout years that lasted.)

Life teaches us sometimes that things are not black and white.

There is a lot of grey. Grey increases to fade more of the black and darken the white. Lists and plans are grey and can be changed in a flash.

A sudden thunderstorm, missing a request in a contract rider, a resignation, an election, emergency surgery, and many other possibilities can change our plans.

Our former pastor friend reminded me that we make plans, God makes plans, and guess Who wins?

I know that I cannot plan out all of 2024. I cannot change the events of the last sixty years. I can, however, make the best of each day.

I can take deep breaths (not too rapidly, so there is no hyperventilation). I can lean on fellow volunteers. I can offer assistance to colleagues and others in need.

I will do what I espouse to my grandchildren: do the best I can every day. No more, no less, just the best for that day. I cannot expect perfection (I used to try!), but I recognise that every day's best may differ. Today's best may pale compared to yesterday's highs, but that is OK.

I started this chapter quite some time ago but 'shredded' the contents as it didn't suit where I am. 2023 has been topsy-turvy (gross understatement). I allowed the roller coaster ride to overwhelm me and cause me to lose focus on my personal goals (my writing, for one).

No matter the chaos around me, I shall continue to do my best day by day.

I choose to strengthen my past delegation abilities so that I do not feel as overwhelmed when life grants yet more surprises. I need to be stronger and kinder to those around me, from my husband to grandchildren, fellow volunteers to friends, and professional acquaintances to persons yet unmet.

I am determined not to permit those with various tendencies (passive-aggressive, narcissistic, and others) to win at manipulation, change my focus, or wither my strengths. This sounds like a negative closing to my chapter. That is not the intent!

I remind you that there is always some ugliness somewhere around us, ready to throw us off course. We cannot know what leads certain people to yield to negative objectives, but we need not follow those paths ourselves.

My tagline at the end of 2023 is “I’m pretending to be fabulous!”

I may not be fabulous. I may not even feel fabulous. Wise friends recently reminded me that I need to make sure I manifest my personal positivity in my own speech.

I shall not pretend things are good around me when they are not.

I will face the negative, plod my way through it, weather the storm, and move on. I will remind myself that there is always light at the end of the tunnel.

And I shall dance.

Am I a successful woman? That probably depends on your definition of success. We all view success differently. I have moments of success and moments of learning from mistakes.

I know that I can conquer that which is set before me. Rome was not built in a day. Nor was I.

Recognising strengths and weaknesses and working with both is a success. Physical pain may continue to haunt me, but *I plan to rock on out each and every year to come!*

“

I know my worth. I embrace my power. I say if I'm beautiful. I say if I'm strong. You will not determine my story. I will.

AMY SCHUMER

SARA NYSTROM

2024

CHAPTER 16

Success Through Intuition, Faith and Resilience

By Sara Nystrom

After Rain Comes Sun: Faith

March 22nd, 2022. The tranquilisers I requested don't seem to be taking effect, even with the double dose. The wall clock ticks down to twenty minutes to nine, and the nurses are approaching to take me to surgery. These could be my final moments. The hug I shared with my eight-year-old son last night, as he and his dad visited me at the hospital, might have been the last one. The video call with my family, too. But I can't dwell on that now. I must focus—on my faith, on being brave.

Beneath the sheets, my legs shiver, whether from fear or the cold, I can't discern. I remind myself to be courageous. In my head, a fear more intense than any I've felt before, but in my heart, an unusual calm. I have faith. I can't know if I'll survive the high-risk neurosurgery ahead, but something within me just knows.

Fully aware of the numerous risks—death, brain infarct, stroke, speech difficulties, damaged vision, paralysis—I push those thoughts away. I tell myself to focus on what I want, not what I don't want. I think about my beautiful life, envision it the way I desire. And I reflect on the incredible contributions I want to make to this world, a life purpose recently discovered. Just before the anesthesia mask descends, I make a promise to the Universe, to God, and to all the angels watching over me—I'll contribute to a better world if I make it through.

The surgery, anticipated to take seven hours, has me waking up a mere three hours later. A purposeful awakening, I sense. No fatigue or nausea; instead, an indescribable sense of bliss and joy. My immediate thought is gratitude to the surgeons and to higher powers, weaving a sense of spirituality into the profound gratitude that envelops me.

After rain comes sun, they say. This is my story of rain and sun. As I pen these words, I wonder if it all truly happened to me. It did. Every word is true. The unthinkable occurred, and I share it with you because I want you to believe that anything is possible. *Our greatest challenges can transform into our most significant successes.*

It's often said that behind every great success story lies a challenge, a struggle. I've come to believe it's there to prepare us, to make us stronger. My narrative is about finding the courage to follow our hearts, a daunting yet rewarding endeavour. Listening to our heart's voice and having the courage to heed it are crucial elements of success.

The Awakening: Following My Heart

My journey began in 2018 when I attended Tony Robbins' "Unleash the Power Within" program in London. Despite financial constraints, an inner voice insisted I attend. That decision changed my life.

On the first night of the UPW event, I walked on fire alongside 13,000 fellow participants—a symbolic act to conquer our fears. The following day brought a profound connection with myself, a depth I had never experienced before, accompanied by unstoppable tears. Outwardly, I had a successful life—a flourishing career with managerial responsibilities and a decent salary, a stable relationship, and a son we had adopted three years earlier. We also had a beautiful house we had just finished renovating.

Yet, an unsettling feeling persisted. I sensed something was amiss, an unclear sensation that occasionally surfaced. It wasn't tangible and certainly not easy to comprehend. I seemingly had it all, right? However, my heart wasn't happy; only my mind was.

In hindsight, those moments of dissatisfaction were my heart whispering to me. It had been attempting to communicate for a while, but I ignored its messages, dismissing them as illogical and nonsensical.

Attending the UPW event in April 2018 felt like a wake-up call. I realised I needed to change my life, including ending my current relationship and leaving my job. However, I wasn't ready for such significant changes. Major transformations require time to mature. Regarding my relationship, I resorted to a common tactic when insights are too painful—I buried my head in the sand, pretended all was well, and forged ahead. I skillfully ignored those persistent whispers from my heart.

I enrolled in a global Business Mentorship Program, committing to absorbing everything about business. While I had decided to start my own company, the specific area remained unknown. These were the initial steps toward running my own business.

By the end of 2018, I launched my first business. A year later, I resigned from my job. Admittedly, I wasn't entirely ready, but I was done with that job and felt a burning desire to sever ties definitively. So, I did exactly that. I threw twelve years of secure employment out the window and celebrated. As if these changes weren't enough, I unexpectedly found the conviction, certainty, and courage to follow my heart in my relationship.

Just two weeks later, the world was hit by the COVID-19 pandemic, leading to the closure of my business. I wasn't prepared for this abrupt shift. Stripped of employment and business, I had no choice but to seek a job. And so, I did. Little did I know that every challenge carries the seed of a new opportunity.

The Journey Unfolding: Resilience

It was the beginning of 2020, and suddenly, from one day to another, I found myself without employment, a company, or a relationship. Describing those times as challenging is an understatement, yet within my heart, I held a deep trust that everything would work out. I followed an instinct, a knowing without knowing, fuelled by faith.

Evenings became my sanctuary for meditation and prayer, gazing at the stars, uttering the same words each night: "I am ready to give. I am ready to receive."

Since childhood, an inexplicable feeling resided within me—a sense of having a special mission in life, something to do, accomplish, and contribute. However, the exact nature of this mission eluded me, leaving me restless. My quest had led me to explore 70+ countries, live in 10, and learn seven foreign languages. Looking back, these past experiences were all preparations; my life was gearing up for what now lay ahead. Things unfold only when we are ready for them. I believe that the moment we connect with our hearts and find the courage to listen, we become ready to embrace our true purpose.

Here I was, without a job, business, income, or a relationship. Yet, I was doing alright because I stood up for myself. Listening to the whispers of my heart, the more I did, the stronger it became—a voice guiding me.

Despite numerous job applications, for the first time in my life, success eluded me. Perhaps, I think, this was to provide the necessary time to nurture my evolving concept. Gradually, an idea took root in my mind and heart, initially in a different form but unmistakably present.

I continued cohabitating with my ex-husband. The initial sadness of endings lingered, but the foundation of our relationship, built on friendship, remained intact, growing even stronger.

The essence of my 2020 was about following my heart, even when it seemed irrational, and maintaining faith, trusting that everything would be fine, even without understanding why. The year concluded with an unexpected reward.

Being Ready: Timing

The answer to my prayers struck me with the force of lightning. Following a late-night conversation with a friend, it felt as if my hand was autonomously writing, downloading something I inherently carried. The concept of "Communication Queen" and its seven steps hit me with undeniable force. My mission found me; I didn't seek it consciously.

While I had never considered working specifically with women, I embraced it without question. I realised my life had uniquely prepared me to empower women globally, fostering confidence, charisma, and impactful communication.

Suddenly, the restless years spent navigating the world by myself made sense. The confidence, communication skills, negotiation skills, social skills, toughness, perseverance, even language skills—all were components of my preparation. The day I found the courage to listen to my heart marked the first step toward discovering my life purpose and fully connecting with myself, my inner being, my soul.

From that moment onward, my life unfolded like a fairy tale or a movie. It wasn't easy, but it gained momentum at the speed of light. I eagerly shared my new concept on social media and was astonished to see hundreds of likes pouring in from around the world in no time—an unprecedented response. Just 30 minutes later, my phone rang. A connection in Kenya invited me to speak at an online pan-African Women's Conference, an invitation I promptly accepted.

The Rewards of Following the Heart: Things Falling into Place

Following the conference, the organisation's founder reached out to me. She had recognised the passion in my heartfelt speech and extended an offer for me to become the co-founder of a global non-governmental organisation empowering women—the World Women Organization. Guided entirely by my heart at that point, I accepted without giving it a second thought. Little did I know, this decision would open up an entirely new world and pave the way for numerous important connections down the road.

Approximately a month later, I hosted my inaugural Communication Queen online workshop. Once again, I marvelled at the fact that, without any marketing efforts, 70 women from 20+ countries registered, and an impressive 50 of them actively participated. By the end of the workshop, they were already asking when the next one would be, expressing that it was an answer to their prayers and exactly what they needed.

I was overwhelmed with joy. My heart sang, and doubts vanished. I was now certain that I was on the right path. I've come to believe that when things progress rapidly and effortlessly, it's a sign that we are aligned with what we are meant to be doing. However, despite this heart connection and the success of my concept, instant income wasn't guaranteed.

As convinced as I was about finally being on the right path professionally, I realised the need to stabilise my personal life. Securing a job became essential for the bank to grant me the necessary loan to purchase my own place. Co-living with my ex-husband worked well, but ending the relationship had its reasons. I secured a temporary job as a job coach, which not only paid my bills but also put food on the table. Within a few months, I managed to secure a bank loan and acquire a beautiful apartment next to the forest, just 200 meters from my ex-husband's new house. We chose to remain close friends, prioritising our son, who is more important than anything else to both of us.

You might find it surprising or perhaps not, but throughout the entirety of 2020, I visualised all the pieces falling into place—one by one. Remarkably, they did, including my job, my flat, and most significantly, my mission, purpose, and sense of meaningfulness.

Obsessed: Forgetting Myself

In the summer of 2021, I made the move to my new flat. It was only then that we decided to share the news with our son, and surprisingly, it went smoothly. Our loving friendship and lack of drama made it easier for him, and I'm eternally grateful for that in my heart.

With my personal life on track, I could refocus on Communication Queen and my newfound mission. In just two weeks, I penned a book and then crafted an online mentorship program, successfully selling it to my first six clients across five countries. Over eight weeks, we embarked on the Communication Queen journey, traversing seven transformative steps. The results began manifesting within weeks, accompanied by incredible feedback and testimonials. One client, overwhelmed with gratitude for her breakthroughs, even recorded a 14-minute video.

It marked a significant success! My journey took me to Nigeria, where I received the prestigious "Most Inspiring Woman of the Year" award. Momentum was building rapidly. Over two years, I had orchestrated a complete life overhaul — divorce, career change, flat purchase and renovation, book authorship, creation, sale, and teaching of my online program. The pace was intense, a testament to my dedication. However, every achievement came at a cost.

Admittedly, I lived solely for my mission and my son during this period. I breathed it, neglecting proper nutrition, adequate sleep, exercise, and a social life. It was a sacrifice, one that concerned my family, who worried about my health and well-being. Despite their concerns, and blinded by my determination, I pressed on.

Then, the unexpected occurred — my accident. This brings us to the story's beginning. On a skiing holiday with my son on February 28th, 2022, I fell and hit my head. Despite wearing a helmet and navigating a mild slope at a moderate speed, I experienced a subarachnoid hemorrhage and a cerebral aneurysm — a critical condition. The mortality rate for such an event has been estimated as high as 60-80%, and among those who survive, only 10-20% recover fully.

Resurging: Combining My Mission with My New Wiser Me

After five weeks in three different hospitals, a high-risk neurosurgery, and an extended sick leave, I emerged in 2023 not only recovering physically but also reclaiming myself from the tumultuous years.

Although my physical recovery was remarkably swift, I allowed myself the necessary time for emotional and psychological healing. While I harbour grand ambitions for the mission I'm on, a crucial lesson emerged — to help others, we must first help ourselves. To contribute to a better world, I recognised the importance of being in the right place and prioritising self-care. This profound realisation unfolded throughout the year 2022, bringing with it a wealth of learning and growth.

In 2023, I experienced a profound resurgence. It was intense, challenging, and demanded hard work, yet this time, I made a conscious effort not to lose sight of myself.

The culmination of my efforts materialised as I finally launched my book, embracing the author within me. The book found its place on prominent platforms such as Amazon, Waterstones, and the Rovingheights bookstore chain in Nigeria. An exciting chapter unfolded as I collaborated closely with Tony Robbins and his team in the UK. Simultaneously, I took the significant step of recording my Mentorship Program. Two trips to Nigeria marked the beginning of incredible partnerships with influential world-changers, including royalties, politicians, an archbishop, senior pastors, and other influential figures. The year 2023 bestowed upon me the honour of receiving another two prestigious awards — "Women's Empowerer of the Year" and the "Global Influencer Award," along with a Yoruba Chieftaincy title. It was during this year that I took the initial strides to establish my international Communication Queen team.

Reflecting on the past five years, I recognise the journey as one of profound self-awareness and relentless self-development. Though arduous, it now appears as the necessary rain preceding the sun, a series of challenges designed to propel me toward following my heart and emerging stronger than ever. At this juncture, I stand more prepared than ever before, carrying the unwavering faith that 2024 will be my most successful year to date. This enduring faith, cultivated along the journey, remains my steadfast companion, a trust that has become an integral part of who I am.

Lessons Learnt: My Journey to Success

As this chapter concludes, I reflect on the profound lessons that have shaped my transformative journey over the past five years. It has been a journey characterised by resilience, positivity, unwavering faith, and the courage to follow my heart.

Following My Heart: The cornerstone of my transformation has been the commitment to listen to the whispers of my heart. These subtle nudges, once ignored, are now the guiding force behind my decisions, leading me to a life aligned with my true purpose. Our hearts may seem crazy, but they are the true temples of our wisdom, while our minds serve to shield us from fears, many of which are not even real.

Positivity as a Driving Force: Amidst challenges and setbacks, maintaining a positive mindset has been pivotal. It's not about denying difficulties but acknowledging them while nurturing an optimistic outlook, which has been a beacon illuminating the darkest paths. Positive energy attracts positive things, and it played a crucial role in my survival—a story in itself!

Confidence as a Catalyst: Cultivating the power within has been essential. Confidence, the silent ally in my pursuits, has empowered me to step into unknown territories, create opportunities, and embrace challenges as avenues for growth.

Resilience in the Face of Adversity: Every setback has been a setup for a comeback. The resilience cultivated during moments of adversity has been instrumental. Instead of viewing challenges as roadblocks, I've learnt to see them as stepping stones toward greater achievements.

Unyielding Faith: Faith has been the constant companion, an anchor during storms. Whether navigating personal relationships or professional endeavours, this steadfast faith has allowed me to weather uncertainties and emerge stronger on the other side.

Continuous Learning: Embracing a mindset of continuous learning has been crucial. Each experience, whether triumphant or challenging, is a lesson. This commitment to growth has fuelled my evolution, making me more adaptable and open to new possibilities.

Authenticity: The power of authenticity cannot be overstated. Being true to myself has not only fostered genuine connections but has also been the magnetic force attracting opportunities aligned with my values.

Gratitude: Amidst the pursuit of goals, I've discovered the profound impact of gratitude. It is the cornerstone of contentment, a reminder to appreciate the journey and the people who have played a role in it.

As I stand on the precipice of a new chapter, I carry these lessons as my guiding light. The combination of following my heart, maintaining positivity, fostering resilience, exuding confidence, and having unshakable faith has paved the way for the successes I've achieved thus far.

With each step forward, I am poised to embrace the future with open arms, confident that the transformative journey continues to unfold, revealing new facets of growth and possibilities.

My Heartfelt Message to You

As you embark on your own journey of self-discovery and transformation, remember that challenges, though disguised as obstacles, are often the very gifts that make you stronger. Embrace them with open arms, for within each challenge lies an opportunity for growth and resilience.

Be the architect of your own happiness. Take responsibility for the joy that colours your days, and know that your happiness is a reflection of the choices you make and the way you choose to perceive the world around you.

Cherish and love yourself unconditionally. Recognise the unique tapestry of talents and gifts that you carry within, for they are the essence of your being. You are beautiful just the way you are, a masterpiece in constant evolution.

In moments of doubt or uncertainty, open your heart. Let it be your guide through the twists and turns of life. Trust in the process, knowing that each step, whether forward or backward, is a vital part of your personal journey.

Gratitude is a magic elixir that transforms the ordinary into the extraordinary. Be grateful for the lessons, the people, and the experiences that shape your path. In expressing gratitude, you invite more blessings into your life.

As I pen these words, I can confidently say that I will never regret embarking on this transformative journey. It has unfolded in unexpected ways, revealing the strength that resides within and the endless possibilities that await those who dare to follow their hearts.

May your journey be filled with moments of profound self-discovery, unwavering faith, and the joy that comes from living an authentic and purposeful life. Trust in the beauty of your own becoming, and remember, the magic happens when you believe in yourself.

You are the author of your story, and every chapter is an opportunity for growth, love, and boundless fulfillment.

Your Success Blueprint for 2024: 12 Principles to Transform Your Journey

1. Follow your heart, be brave, and listen to its whispers.
2. Our minds often shield us from unfounded fears.
3. Assistance arrives when we follow our hearts.
4. Believe in yourself, especially when others don't.
5. Stand up for your happiness, taking responsibility for self-love.
6. Challenges foster growth and preparation.
7. Timing is crucial; be patient, things happen when they're meant to.
8. Practice optimism, gratitude, and visualisation.
9. Surround yourself with like-minded individuals.
10. Contribute authentically, build your business on passion.
11. Connect heart-to-heart, attract positive energy.
12. Get mentors and continually expand your network.

May these principles light your path to success in the coming year! Trust that intuition, faith, resilience, optimism, and inner power are skills that can be cultivated and evolved. I've personally undergone this journey, and through Communication Queen, I empower women worldwide to do the same. *If I can evolve these qualities, so can you.*

With much love, warmth, and a firm belief in your journey,

Sara Nystrom
Communication Queen
Stockholm, December 26, 2023

SUE BLACKWELL

2024

CHAPTER 17

Turning the World Upside Down

By Sue Blackwell

What gives me, a humble musician, the right to boldly write a chapter in a book about successful women?

I've been on an extraordinary adventure these past 42 years with my family. We transform the lives of people all too often forgotten by society. We turn perceived norms upside down. We have big ambitions to reach further and wider into every corner of the world.

I am a mum on a mission! I am indignant because the medics saw fit to write my first-born child off at birth. With no warning, after a textbook pregnancy, we were labelled a disabled family five hours after Jen was born. We were told she wouldn't amount to much and it would be best to put her in a home and forget about her.

But why shouldn't Jen have the same opportunities to be herself and share her love and talents with others? Just because she has Down's Syndrome, why shouldn't Jen follow her dreams of being a dance leader in her community?

Why shouldn't Jen and people with learning disabilities have access to support and encouragement to lead a life of their choosing and do what brings them joy?

I write BECAUSE of Jen, her dance, her focus and passion for life, and her learning disability. Unbeknownst to me, Jen had already started making me my own person. As a natural introvert, Jen forced me to step up on her behalf, to be assertive where she wasn't able to be, to reach out to others, and not be afraid to ask for help.

If you measure success financially, I'm not off the starting blocks, having chosen to work as a volunteer for almost all my working life. If, however, we look at the legacy of our lives, I would be happy to be nominated posthumously for the yet-to-be-coined 'Queen of Tenacity and Successful Actions' award, but only if open to joint applicants as it would necessarily include Jen, my award-winning, decorated daughter, who happens to have Down's syndrome.

I'm told I think differently to most people. My default setting is to seek creative solutions to the multiple challenges life presents each and every one of us.

I invite you to believe in the possibility of creating a different society. One where every person matters, no matter who they are, what they look like or what their perceived abilities are. I believe everyone can contribute with joy to their family and community in their lives.

I want to challenge and change perceptions of what's possible for people with a learning disability or marginalised in some way. They are often pushed around by systems that make no sense to those they are supposed to serve or those who work within the constraints of a checklist.

I know there's a different way from my personal experience of simply listening to my daughter. From her basic needs to support her in becoming the inspiring motivational speaker she naturally is, leading a multi-award-winning charity, recognised in 2023 in the Kings Honours list for her services to disabled people.

The system sought to marginalise Jen from the off. We were referred to the Child Development Unit in the local town. I turned up to the clinical environment where Jen, just a few months old, was weighed, measured, 'assessed' and fussed over by other mums. Then a 7-year-old girl approached us with her tongue lolling down her chin, wanting to cuddle Jen too roughly for my liking, followed by the loudest wakeup call I could possibly have received from her mum, 'she can't help it; she's got Down's syndrome'. At that moment, if I hadn't known it before, I knew I couldn't accept the status quo of a fundamentally flawed system that cannot serve each person. All of us are.

Already actively searching libraries for knowledge and different thinking, at 5 months old, we flew to Detroit to meet an alternative doctor working with nutritional therapy; at 6 months, we visited the British Institute for Brain Injured Children to learn more; at 9 months we embarked on a daily structured developmental program of cross-patterning BIBIC prescribed bringing support and order to our lives.

Starting with 3 hours a day, over the months and years, the activities' frequency, intensity, and duration transformed Jen from a person who could not move from A to B to a person who could crawl up a six-foot-long ramp within three months. We were surrounded by incredible local people who volunteered to help with the daily exercises and brought hope, inspiration and happiness to our home. This is the febrile atmosphere into which Anthony was born, who joined Jen in the exercises, crawling, singing, laughing and having fun.

Later, after relocating, the local authority chose to steer Jen towards the special school in a different town, to be picked up and returned by taxi. They had a spare place they wanted to fill. We felt strongly that Jen had the right to be educated in her community, mix with others, pursue her interests in swimming and brownies, and dance alongside others she knew from her village and school.

I've always sought to do my best as a mum, and from day one, I never wanted to look in the mirror and say, 'I could have tried harder'. As Jen's parents, we've found our way, step by tentative step, unsure and unclear, always listening to ourselves and our children. We believe each of our children is their own person and have always encouraged them to follow their dreams. Jen (42) is a dancer and musician, and Anthony (40) is an engineer.

Perhaps we are experts by experience now, but I prefer 'professionals'. As professionals, we have an important contribution to make from those inauspicious beginnings. As parents/caregivers, we don't necessarily need to be experts, but we are professionals in the lives of our loved ones. We know what feels right or when we're being pushed into something that ticks someone else's box.

Respecting and supporting each other to be the best that we can be, recognising each of us has an equal right to contribute, each voice is valid, and being involved and supporting each other on our journeys through life are fundamental to Malcolm and I. Practising what we now know to be termed co-production.

Our brand of co-production permeates all areas of our lives. None of the 4 of us would be living as we do without the support of each other and without the support of Jen's dedicated care team or **DanceSyndrome**. Each is a part of the whole system of support and won't work without the other parts' contribution, existence, or support.

Co-production happens naturally when underpinned by a bedrock of inclusion, and inclusion only occurs when people are respected and valued for the person they are. That only occurs when we learn to listen and communicate in a way that shows we are listening.

There is absolutely no point in sitting down with Jen for a serious discussion of any length without being open to interjections of dance. Whenever I hear 'Mum, can I ask you something?' or 'I know they're a special friend, but ....' it's time to down tools, to listen attentively to what's being said (and what's not being said), to be present in the moment, to gift the time to seek to help to find solutions through the challenge Jen is striving to unravel, but struggling to make sense of. And when nothing seems to be working, recognise that sometimes you need to reach out to others – carers, family members, friends, or professionals – that's okay.

Jen's dream was always to dance. She danced everywhere, so it made absolute sense that this would be her vision for the future. At the age of 18, an adult in the eyes of the law, the system expected Jen to pick up a thread with no support.

At age 21, a frustrated Jen threw down the challenge to us and society: "I live for dance – it's my passion and my life. I have the right to a life of my choosing. My future lies in dance. I want to share my passion for dance and get the world dancing." 20 years on, Jen will tell you: "I'm living my best life in dance. My disability doesn't define who I am."

After 10 years of searching high and low, we realised that the training we sought didn't exist. And that it wasn't only Jen who was being made to feel like they didn't belong in a society that saw people with learning disabilities as an inconvenience.

Nobody offered exactly what she needed – an inclusive structured opportunity spanning several years, where she could be treated equally and with appropriate support around her.

I remember the People Dancing conference in 2002 as a turning point. 200 plus community dancers confirmed that the training we sought didn't exist anywhere in the UK. We finally knew we weren't alone. It allowed us to be innovative and creative without facing rejection and closed doors. Those early days weren't easy. We attempted to work with a couple of dancers in different ways. Also, we tried alternative living/caring arrangements for Jen to become more independent, but eventually, she returned to our family home, broken by the system. With no gainful daytime activity, no dance training or dancers in her life, and, despite a huge number of acquaintances, not one real friend, Jen was hurting badly.

That's when we knew things had to change, and we had to take responsibility for making change happen. Our charity DanceSyndrome was set up out of frustration with the system. Ten years on, it is now also a multi-award winner, impacting the lives of thousands of people.

Without Jen, there would be no DanceSyndrome. But without DanceSyndrome to support them, Jen and her peers would be casualties of the system, kept out of sight and out of mind.

At DanceSyndrome, diversity is the norm, and inclusion is our bedrock - there are no barriers or hurdles to clear or glass ceilings to break through – everybody matters and has something to offer the conversation.

DanceSyndrome will always be grounded in the ethos that everyone matters. We are in demand. We are contributing to society. People are finding the support they need, whether it's dance, a social outlet, or a fun activity with a friend. People with and without learning disabilities, carers and parents are seeing what's possible for everyone.

Our unique business and delivery model is being recognised for its impact. We're recognised as change leaders, creating an impact wherever we go. We make a difference through our workshops and training programs across all sectors. At universities, we get under the skin of undergraduates before they embark on their careers, influencing and changing their perceptions and assumptions about people with learning disabilities and delivering seminars they will never forget.

From being written off, Jen, her friends and the support team, all co-contributors to DanceSyndrome, make it look so easy! I won't tell you about the extra struggles we've faced because of our unique co-production model. You know the ups and downs that anyone who creates an impact and/or grows a business to make a difference in your community faces. Add a learning disability into the mix, and you'll get the picture.

Just imagine living in a world where discrimination doesn't exist, where every person brings their unique talents and assets to the table, taking from it what they need to nourish their soul, to flourish and thrive. Jointly, we build the community of 'us', a place and space where everyone belongs.

I never knew what was possible until i challenged and turned things upside down. I know i've helped my daughter and son in their journey to become the unique people they are. Thinking differently is our norm as we live 'the art of the possible' through daily life and the strength and growth of dancesyndrome.

We all have choices in life. Or do we? We cannot and shouldn't make assumptions about others. The choices i've made may be very different from the choices you've made, probably dictated by circumstances such as family issues, mental health, disability, age, illness, financial security, etc. Our blinkered vision of learning disabilities gets in the way of allowing jen to fulfil her dream. We assume she can't be the visionary she craves to be because of her learning disability, so we don't give her a chance.

If we pare it down to basics, DanceSyndrome began with Jen's dream:-

A dancer with learning disabilities craving equity (EQUALITY OF OPPORTUNITY)

A leader from unexpected places (DIVERSITY)

Including every person in the way that works for them (INCLUSION)

Wanting and needing the support of insightful others (CO-PRODUCTION)

Sharing and contributing to spreading happiness, joy and well-being in her wake (BEING HUMAN)

Jen herself will tell you **'the best outcome of all is friendship.** I hadn't discovered friendship before DanceSyndrome, but now I have friends - people who value me for who I am - it's the most amazing experience ever!"

What's stopping Jen from fulfilling her dream? Learning disability or attitudes? Because she has learning disabilities, she is deemed to be incapable of leading or contributing. Perhaps she might have found opportunities to work as an assistant or a helper with a dance artist, but that wasn't what she wanted. She wanted to lead. Her words and body language gave voice to this message loudly and clearly. She engaged people in her dance everywhere she went with no verbal skills required. Jen's passion has shone through all her life.

So what can we do? What must we do? We can change the narrative – you, me, your next-door neighbour. We can step up, surpass that invisible divide, embrace the human being within and discover what is important to them. Find out what that person is interested in, passionate about, intrigued by, or incredibly good at – which might be sitting still – and then harness their power imaginatively. Open doors where they can't by themselves, walk beside them, allow them to reach you, listen, gift time, and before you know it, you'll have a new friend who will intrigue you, empower you, guide you to new horizons, teach you things you'd never previously considered, and quite possibly you will have found a friend for life and new different opportunities to explore yourself. Your life will be richer BECAUSE of thinking differently.

My eutopia exists – a place where people are experiencing indescribable joy by being recognised for who they are – a human being.

Together, we make a difference. We can transform lives and break down barriers, enabling people to follow their dreams and passions and show that everyone matters. Turning things upside down creates possibilities and unexpected outcomes for everyone.

SUE POWELL

2024

CHAPTER 18

Are You Sitting Comfortably?

By Sue Powell

Hi, my name is Sue Powell; my story begins when my youngest brother, Simon, was born. There were eleven years between us, and it was a big shock to me and my other brothers. Helping to look after him began a natural love of looking after children and ended up as an interesting, successful career. I originally wanted to be a teacher but did not get the required A-level results, so I got steered into nursery nursing by my lovely mum. I think I took after her as she was like a magnet to children, which could have been down to the amount of sweets/ treats she used to keep in her pockets.

In about 1995, when my own child James was three years old, I had a chest infection; after 6 months, I still felt exhausted and ill and was diagnosed with M.E./ chronic fatigue or how it used to be called "yuppy flu." It completely changed my life; my energy levels hit an all-time low. Picture walking upstairs and feeling as if you had completed a 10-mile trek. I struggled with painful, swollen joints and muscles, became very depressed, anxious, frustrated and had no motivation. Eventually, I came to terms with my diagnosis and the fact that I could not physically do the same things that I used to. I remember being referred to a hospital in London, using all my energy to go down there on the train. I had blood tests, had to fill in lots of questionnaires, was asked lots of questions and at the end of it, I said, "Well, there is no magic cure." How debilitating and crushing that was, I knew there was no magic cure, but some kind words might have been better. I remember going home feeling even more depressed than before. It's a good lesson in how your words can make such a difference in a person's life and alter it for better or worse.

I have tried all sorts of supposed cures for M.E., such as CBT, acupuncture, aloe vera gel, etc, which are expensive and so could only be afforded for a short time. You can join M.E. groups online, but after reading a few comments, I felt that they would pull my mood down even further, so I have always avoided them. I am sure for some people, they are a lifeline, just not for me. One of the best pieces of advice is to pace yourself daily. There are days when I have more energy and feel like I want to do everything, but if I do lots of activities and overdo them, I end up suffering and not being able to get out of bed for days afterwards. It has taken me a long time to learn these lessons, and I still don't always listen to my body enough. But if I ignore them and try to push through, I end up with burnout and must take time off work.

I have had a very interesting career working as a nanny both in the U.K. and Switzerland, in day nurseries and schools, and as an assistant director in a nanny agency. Then, joining the NHS in 2000, I worked with additional needs children, school nursing and most recently, health visiting with families of 0–5-year-olds.

I love my job and feel very passionate about helping children and families, but I still suffer from joint pains and anxiety. I have had to learn to hold some energy back and not give everything to my job, and sometimes, I must just stop the world, get off and rest a while to let my body and mind recover. I would not wish M.E. or any chronic illness on anybody, but if there are any positives, it would be that I can empathise/ talk to parents who might be going through similar experiences. It has taught me that I am a strong person who tries to look on the positive side even when feeling under par; helping others and being non-judgemental can bring much more to your life.

During my M.E. I found writing, I have always been drawn to creative activities and discovered that putting pen to paper relaxes me, declutters my mind and creates something wonderful. The messages in my books are meant to be shared, enjoyed, questioned and hopefully help some children and parents. Although I love my job in the NHS, my "gifted job" as a children's author brings me much more excitement, pleasure and satisfaction. As a nursery nurse, I have read hundreds of books to different groups of children. Imagine the pleasure and pride of sitting in front of those eager, curious faces, reading my books and trying to answer their probing questions such as "How old are you?" I also leave the children with the message that we are all important, we all matter, and we all bring something unique to this world (sadly, not my words, but from The Boy, the Mole, the Fox and the Horse by Charlie Mackesy), a book I love.

I have made some toy characters for my latest book “Mixed Veg” and look forward to using them to help tell my story to my audiences. Children love humour in books, so mucking around is mandatory in my readings.

Even at 65, I still have a very childlike and silly sense of humour; I like to bring my quirky sense of humour to work when appropriate and hope that my laughter therapy has brought a smile to someone’s face. If you can have a giggle, it makes everything else in life bearable and I know that my sense of humour, albeit sometimes weird and nutty, has helped me through some dark times.

In 2024, I intend to use my energy and skills on networking, promotion, writing more books and spending more time mixing with my tribe.

TRACEY-JANE HUGHES
2024

CHAPTER 19

Finding the Course to Listen

By Tracey-Jane Hughes

With my head on my unforgivingly hard desk, feeling like an utter failure, in a cold rented unit surrounded by rails of bras for sale and boxes from our house move, I wanted to jump off the world. I felt guilty about my decisions over the past 5 years. I couldn't do this anymore. I couldn't go on pretending that I was OK. I didn't want to be in this place surrounded by memories of the exponential highs before the credit crunch of 2008, which halved my sales in the first month.

How could I have been awarded "Business Mum of the Year" when my life fell apart? I couldn't recreate the expansion, the excitement or even the connection I'd had with my business and, worse still, with the customers I'd set the business up to support. I was exhausted and wanted to hide under my duvet and let the world go on without me. I had no energy to deal with this monster I'd created.

That's when I heard it. The soft and insistent voice whispered kindly, "Let it go". I knew I had to let go of the business I'd built from scratch when my youngest son was three months old. I knew that for the sake of my own health, it was time to move on.

As a busy business owner, trainer, coach, Mum, taxi, carer, cook, shopper and all those other roles I took on in my family and community, I realised with a blinding flash that I wasn't listening to myself. I was too busy doing things, ticking things off my "to do" list, ensuring my boys had PE kit and healthy food to eat, juggling the washing and speaking with coaching clients, fitting in training sessions for bra fitters, and updating my website and social media.

It took another couple of years to really start listening consciously and change the course of my life and that of my family, friends and clients. I was shown my first step when a friend asked me to become a listening trainer for their volunteer listening service.

I used to think I was clever doing everything on my list and juggling my business and family commitments. The freedom I've experienced since committing to listening more has transformed my life. Only by listening to ourselves can we really be successful in our lives.

I remember getting to the point where I was focusing for so many hours, but nothing was working. I felt like there was a secret handshake I hadn't been shown that was the key to success for the next phase of my life. Everyone else was doing OK; why did I feel like such a failure again? What jigsaw piece was missing from my knowledge or experience? Where was the magical, missing memo that hadn't reached me yet?

I was exhausted. I was tired of being the central cog. I wasn't sleeping well. My body felt wonky, and everything I did seemed to clash against something else. There was no rhythm beating an easy step in my week. I wanted to leave the world and allow it to turn without me. But I couldn't do that as I'd made myself the core hub in the system of our family.

As I felt my joints jarring on the pavements on my twice-weekly runs, I knew my exhausted body was trying to tell me something wasn't right. My constantly whirring mind was depriving me of vital sleep. I was trying to figure out how to complete the 5D puzzle, getting everything I'd committed to do into place without dropping a piece. I needed to be an octopus to hold all the pieces, but I was tying myself in knots.

Not only did I feel the weight of my family's expectations, but I felt like a fraud. Again. I was teaching and coaching others to listen to themselves and take steps to improve their lives, but my body wasn't functioning in a sustainable way. I literally felt like I was falling apart at the seams.

I couldn't go on. Weighted down, feeling stuck in a rut, self-sabotaging. I was letting people down, unable to be fully involved in life because I was exhausted. My head, heart and body seemed to pull me in different directions. I was grumpy and no longer happy in my own skin.

This wake-up call made me understand that I was listening to the needs of others but not my own. I had to listen to my body and take the action it needed. I'd learnt, from my exploration of listening, that everything in our lives is interconnected. I needed help. My first appointment with a naturopath was life-changing and helped me on so many levels.

What I was eating affected my body and mind as much as sleep, exercise and breathing fresh air. He's a true holistic therapist, using kinesiology, nutritional supplements, and chiropractic adjustments and making connections to the natural world I'd never encountered. On that first day, he thought he'd have my body back in alignment within a few weeks. It took two years and included some dentistry adjustments to realign my jaw which was constantly putting my body under stress and making me feel wonky!

The experience of working in this holistic way opened me up to new awareness about myself. I listened more to my body and noticed the smallest physical changes. I realised when I was off balance and became quicker at understanding what was causing it – nutrition, sleep, exercise, work, rest, or how I responded to external situations. The more I learned to listen, the more I discovered connections between mind, body and spirit, realising that I could impact my life by adjusting my thoughts or lifestyle.

We can't just work on aligning our skeletal system, as one tweak impacts the emotional centres of the body and the connective tissue between the joints. Every chakra and meridian connects everything internally first before our energy flows outwards, connecting to everything in our beautiful world.

I learned to listen more deeply to my body and breath. I listened to my negative thoughts and realised there was even more to listening than I'd previously been practising. I couldn't simply heal my body and have more energy; I had to work on all aspects of myself - mind, body and spirit - to ensure every part of me was working together. Our body-mind-spirit can be a well-oiled machine. If we look after them, they'll guide us on an easier path than the one we often stride along unconsciously.

One of the most powerful changes I made to support my mind-spirit was committing to *The Four Agreements* shared by Don Miguel Ruiz in his book of the same name:

- Be impeccable with your word (including thoughts);

- Do not take anything personally;

- Do not make assumptions;

- Always do your best.

Easier said than done, but once I took responsibility for my thoughts and actions, I found peace. Knowing I can't change other people or the circumstances I see myself in but can alter how I react is as freeing as a deep chiropractic adjustment of my twisted neck.

I have needed the courage to take the steps I have. When I'm listening well, I can feel every cell of my body shouting, "Yes, you're listening! Now, here's your next step."

I've allowed myself to explore new ideas and ways of living my life by listening daily to what serves me. Despite the masks of life's challenges and the emotions that still flood me, my body, mind and spirit agree that I have the courage to listen to make choices that are in my best interest. When living in this place, I can support others, be courageous, and listen to what is right for them.

I now choose courage, knowing that change is inevitable every day. Taking responsibility for my health and thoughts, knowing they are all interconnected, has enabled me to feel free to be myself. Even when the steps felt too much, too far, and too expensive, by listening to my body-mind-spirit, I've found new paths, new clients and new ideas flowing to allow me to do what I needed. Even though, on the outside, sometimes it looked like my life was falling apart, I know and have felt through every cell in my body that my life has been falling together.

I know what it's like to feel stuck in an impossible situation without knowing how to hold your head up. It's a place I've moved on from, and I can help you move on too. I am here to listen to you, support you, and help you thrive.

I encourage you to take your next steps with confidence. Listen.

“

I am learning every day to allow the space between where I am and where I want to be to inspire me and not terrify me.

TRACEE ELLIS ROSS

WAIRIMU WAROBI
2024

CHAPTER 20

Principles Stand. Methods Vary

By Wairimu Warobi

We are as unique as our message and our abilities to serve people. My words are purpose and metanoia. I am a born encourager and builder of people.

Have you had life throw curve balls, lobbed so fast you barely breathe? It could be in business, health, family, career, or all of them. You sit on the floor, shattered, hidden from the world. One day, you wake up and realise you are winning in the dark.

Walk along with me, I must attend a long overdue meeting. Dressed in jeans, an African print shirt, and a set of gold loops, I walk into my living room and sit on "the throne." I close my eyes and wait; I do not know how long. A tentative soft voice speaks, "Hi!" "Strange how we do not recognise our own voices." Two friends meet, and the same brown eyes search each other. If you look carefully, you see the sadness. Sitting across me, dressed in jeans and a striped tank top, is Nimo, in her mid-twenties. "It's been a while; you forgot me!" I hear the anxiety, and I start crying. "How are you?" we speak simultaneously. "It has been hard, really hard" I answer. My eyes widen as I watch her. She is the queen of masks, a deeply sensitive soul. I reach into the recesses of her heart and hug her.

What do you want from me"? she asks, "I will tell you soon enough." "Do you have anything to ask me?" "Did we make it?" she asks. "We are 50+!" we chuckle.

"Nimo, sometimes crises are transformational."

"The road you thought you would take does not pan out." "It will be rough for you, yet you become something you never imagined." "What?" "You finally accept, are content and at peace with yourself!" "What does that mean?" "You blossom; you go back to school at 38 choosing topics you like and become a better critical thinker". "You are clear on your identity, principles and values."

"You are an author, a co-author; you write and have featured articles in magazines." "Your bestselling book, "Diary of a Nameless Woman" is a resource book at Lambeth Palace." "You support people with your knowledge." I lean forward and hold her hands, gently rubbing them. "Your heart will be broken; your body will give out; yet you will stumble forward." "What about mum"? I let out a rip-roaring laugh. "She is still a gangster; surprise, she is your best friend." "What happened"? "I took a forgiveness journey." "Are we still close with Dad?" Nimo and I smiled. "That never changes!"

"Why England," she asks. "We were born here, and nomadic feet," she grins. "I love the English language and literature, and London is a cultural feast."

"How are you a published author?" June 16, 2016, whilst shuffling out of a hospital appointment, "The voice, you know the voice," she smiles and says, "Write the book". Instinctively, I knew what I would write about. I became one who creates awareness of mental health and invisible illnesses for Black people. "How?" "Trade union, personal, management experience in the NHS and Social Care." I am selective on who I write for though."

"What about Zuena"? I will write that in time.

"Remember you told Daddy at 10, you would write 5 bestsellers and retire". "When the doctor said I have fibromyalgia, I responded "I am going to reinvent myself." I just did not know to what. "You have changed, how?" she says. After the depression and roller coaster you go through, these are my lessons:

- You must be your own prophet, speak out and listen to yourself.
- Constantly r**eview your Vision and Mission**, especially when there are cataclysmic changes.
- **Invest in yourself**. I signed up for adult education and short courses. My favourite course was "How to Think," which saved me."

- **Manage your thoughts.** "As a man thinketh so is he!"
- **Make the decision, follow through,"** Daddy wisdom. I left a career I loved, a risky financial decision.
- I journal, pointing at two large boxes of journals.
- My mental well-being took precedence. I withdrew and designed a Personal Emotional Evacuation Plan. I engaged in talking therapies to deal with the trauma.
- I listened to doctors, **researched, and took control of my treatment**. Stress and unresolved emotions were triggers to my autoimmune conditions.
- "I prayed, child, I prayed." I went from religious prayers to simple "God help me even in simple tasks like a shower!" I found peace and solitude with The Creator and calmed my system. I went the whole nine yards, spiritual, mental, and physical.

Healing is not linear. I have withdrawn for more than a decade; recovery is more complex than the trauma. I wanted to be a coach/author/speaker, so I had to be realistic in the moment. The diagnosis of depression, infertility, fibromyalgia, lupus, and a nervous breakdown broke me. "I grieve the loss of me." "I nearly died from COVID twice and when Lil'bug left me."

Silent tears drop. "How are you doing with the grief thing"? "Not sure, I miss my little sister so much; I have good and bad days." "Does it get any easier?" "No, I made room for her."

"What about the lupus? Will you die"? "Someday I will, not now; my immune system is suppressed." I assure her, "I am in remission, and it is treatable. I will live a long, healthy life if I do as I am told."

"Are you happy"? she asks, "I don't know what that means." "I am content with me and being differently abled."

"Why did you start with this part of our story?"

I smile thoughtfully, “Over time, what we think are tough times fades, then hell up its ante”! “I want you to know that you are equipped. Every past battle equips you for the next. Your rhesus is RH+ Resilient and Hopeful.”

“What is your plan, and what do you want from me?” she asks. “I want to finish my next two books. “Most of all, I want you to teach me to laugh again.” We stand hugging each other. I close my eyes, and when I open them, she is gone. I hear the flutter of joy at a new adventure and more books.

I've always loved butterflies, because they remind us that it's never too late to transform ourselves.

DREW BARRYMORE

WENDY KIER
2024

CHAPTER 21

ChatGPT: A Catalyst for Change

By Wendy Kier

In my story, I've navigated the challenges of dyslexia, from educational hurdles to facing workplace discrimination and ultimately thriving in my business with ChatGPT's aid. This journey is about resilience, self-empowerment, and embracing technology to transform my professional life, significantly boosting my business. It's a tale of turning obstacles into opportunities, finding confidence in my abilities, and no longer allowing dyslexia to define my limitations.

From Remedial Classes to Resilience: A Tale of Pain, Shame, and Lost Self-Esteem

Imagine having a burning desire to succeed but constantly feeling held back by a learning disability that affects your ability to read and write. This is the reality for millions of people living with dyslexia. This neurological condition makes reading and processing written language a challenge.

My journey with dyslexia has been a tapestry of challenges, often tinged with heartbreak. Let me guide you through the start of it all. My early years were marred by family trauma; my father's struggles with alcoholism led to me being placed under local authority care at the tender age of two. Growing up, I shuffled between numerous foster homes and faced constant upheavals in my schooling. Deemed unable to keep pace with my peers, I was relegated to remedial classes, where it was assumed my turbulent family life impeded my learning. However, the true nature of my struggles remained unnoticed until I was 14 and a half. It wasn't the chaos at home that hindered my education; it was dyslexia. By this point, school support seemed a distant prospect, and I left with only a GCSE in woodwork to my name.

This blend of a traumatic childhood and limited formal education deeply eroded my self-confidence and self-esteem. At 15 and a half, I moved into supportive lodgings, a step to prepare me for independent living. Yet, there I was, grappling with a daunting world and the complexities of managing finances – a challenge compounded by my difficulty with numbers."

I found it challenging to read and write, and I had additional challenges I needed to navigate.

Learning to live independently means that you have to look after your real self. I'm doing things I'm not sure about. I remember it as if I saw yesterday I would have to go into the shop and buy one thing at home cuz I didn't know how to use the money. I couldn't count, so I didn't understand why I would have left. And I was always fearful that I would get it wrong.

The emotional and psychological effects of my experiences were profound. Growing up in a turbulent environment and grappling with undiagnosed dyslexia left me with deep-seated feelings of inadequacy and low self-esteem. The constant changes in my living and schooling situations made me feel unstable and unsupported, fueling a sense of isolation. This was compounded by the frustration and confusion I faced in the classroom, where my learning difficulties were misunderstood. These experiences shaped my outlook and emotional resilience, presenting significant challenges I had to confront and overcome. "Not only were reading and writing monumental challenges, but numeracy was equally daunting. At 15, these hurdles were compounded by the responsibility of managing my finances. The very act of shopping became a stressor, as I struggled with basic transactions due to my inability to count money. This often left me with a persistent fear of making mistakes.

I remember it as if it was yesterday. Managing my weekly allowance was difficult, so I often bought just one item at a time, never quite sure of the cost. The situation was overwhelming. It wasn't just that I didn't recognise the items, but I also struggled to comprehend their pricing. This challenge was a crucial part of learning to live independently.

This is just the beginning of my story. As a woman with dyslexia, I've journeyed through a childhood shadowed by family trauma and academic challenges to mastering independence and financial management. Battling the effects of dyslexia on reading, writing, and numeracy, I've faced and overcome feelings of inadequacy and the fear of errors. My time in foster care and remedial classes sowed seeds of doubt, but through perseverance and resilience, I transformed these into strengths. My story is about unwavering determination and adaptability in facing life's hurdles.

Dyslexia and Discrimination: Losing My Voice in the Workplace

Moving from my educational struggles to independent living and then into the workforce, I encountered new challenges. The transition was anything but smooth, as dyslexia continued to shape my experiences. In professional settings, I had to navigate the complexities of tasks and responsibilities and the often-unseen barriers my learning difficulties posed. I had hoped this part of my story would be easier, but it was much harder, which is difficult to imagine. This section reveals how I grappled with these challenges, finding unique ways to adapt and succeed, and how my journey in the workplace became another crucial step in my personal and professional development.

Within several organisations, I experienced workplace bullying and disability discrimination. It happened not just once but several times, significantly impacting my confidence and self-esteem. In my first job, the manager discovered my dyslexia and fired me on the spot. I had no one to turn to, feeling betrayed and isolated. This further damaged my emotional ability to cope. Without support within the organisations, these experiences left me at risk of homelessness. In one organisation, I transitioned from being a top-level employee to the worst overnight due to a change in management. The new manager constantly put me down, exploiting my dyslexia. With this level of stress, I found myself slipping into depression. I felt hopeless in this situation.

Once I recovered, I started new employment, deliberately choosing a position below my skill set. I pursued an Open University qualification in my own time, but my dyslexia was used against me by my manager and her superior. Faced with unrealistic deadlines and constant demeaning treatment, I reached my breaking point and walked out. This time, I sought the advice of a specialist lawyer in disability discrimination, specifically for dyslexia. The trauma from this loss was so profound that I decided never to be employed again. To avoid further vulnerability, I chose to start my own business.

One of the things I found during this experience was the level of bullying I endured made it impossible to perform at my best. No matter how hard I tried, it felt like I was frozen, paralysed by fear. Despite being the first one into work and the last to leave, my efforts went unnoticed.

As a consequence of my experiences, I found myself losing my voice. I sat in silence in meetings, holding back thoughts for fear of being demeaned. This loss went beyond mere words; it was a loss of my ability to communicate confidently and to express myself in a way that felt understood and accepted. It was a profound silence, a retreat into a space where my words, once vibrant and assertive, became shadows of doubt and apprehension.

I, like many others with dyslexia, am faced in the workplace. These challenges went beyond personal experiences, reflecting widespread issues such as difficulties with reading and writing tasks, organisational struggles, and slower processing times. The story could also address the misconceptions about dyslexia, like underestimating intelligence or assuming a need for less challenging work, and how these impacted my career progression, job satisfaction, and colleague interactions. This context emphasises the need for increased workplace awareness and accommodations for dyslexic employees.

Transform Adversity into Triumph: Discover How Dyslexia Became My Stepping Stone to Success

In my journey through education, independent living, and the workforce, I grappled with dyslexia's unseen barriers. This struggle was not just about tasks and responsibilities; it was a deeper battle for self-confidence and acceptance in the face of workplace bullying and discrimination. Each challenge was a step towards my personal and professional development, leading me to a crucial decision: to embrace my journey and start my own business.

As I turned the page on my experiences with workplace adversity, I embarked on a bold new chapter: launching a coaching and training business. This decision, born from a desire to create a secure and empowering environment for myself, marked a significant shift in my journey. It was a leap into the unknown, fueled by uncertainty and a comprehension of the truth - I didn't know how to do it; I just knew I couldn't put myself back in a situation like that again.

The trauma from my work experiences had a deep psychological impact, and because my self-esteem and self-worth were already little shaped, I struggled to see the value I had to offer. This meant that when I did have work, I didn't charge what I deserved and often over-delivered. I lacked confidence and struggled to get the business off the ground; it took me 8 years. But what other choice did I have but to keep going and try to make a success of it? The alternative was to go back to work and find myself in another bullying situation. I couldn't do that to myself.

As time passed, I discovered that I had a bad relationship with money. It wasn't that I wasn't good at managing money – in fact, I was exceptionally good at it – but it had more to do with how I valued myself. I was already broken because of the childhood trauma I had faced. This was a really challenging time. I also found myself afraid of being criticised.

I found it really difficult to articulate myself. Because I found it hard to articulate and express myself, I could not clearly convey my thoughts and share my voice. The tools I was working with weren't good enough; they didn't help me think and express; they just helped me spell, and honestly, they weren't even good at that.

I would like to say that I overcame the obstacles and could lean into the straps of my dyslexia. Still, the fact is that this is only a recent development truth we know. It's only recently that a significant shift occurred in how I manage my dyslexia. The introduction of ChatGPT into my life marked another turning point, offering a tool that not only aids in overcoming the barriers of dyslexia but also enhances my abilities in ways I never imagined.

This next part of my story delves into the transformative role ChatGPT has played, opening up new avenues for communication, creativity, and business success. It's a journey of embracing technology to thrive in ways I once thought impossible.

Thriving with ChatGPT

My journey with dyslexia has been profoundly transformed by the introduction of ChatGPT into my life and business. This advanced AI language model has not only enhanced my ability to communicate effectively but has also been a cornerstone in overcoming the challenges posed by dyslexia. ChatGPT's text-based communication and editing capabilities have allowed me to express my ideas more coherently, significantly boosting my confidence and professional standing. This transformative technology has been a beacon in my journey, opening doors to new opportunities and enabling me to break down the barriers that dyslexia had once placed in my path.

The impact of ChatGPT on my book-writing process has been nothing short of revolutionary. Before ChatGPT, the process of writing was cumbersome and often fraught with frustrations due to my dyslexia. But with this AI tool, writing became a streamlined and enjoyable process. I could quickly turn thoughts into words, creating content that resonated with my audience. This efficiency led to the rapid publication of several books, greatly accelerating the growth of my coaching business. Each book, filled with valuable insights from my coaching journey, became a powerful tool for sharing knowledge and attracting new clients. The response from readers was overwhelmingly positive, further cementing my confidence in using this tool.

Managing dyslexia in a professional setting has always been a challenge, but ChatGPT has been instrumental in helping me overcome this. The AI's assistance in organising content and refining writing styles has made writing more accessible and less daunting. This technology has revolutionised how I write and played a key role in developing new, innovative services and marketing strategies, further enhancing my business's success. With ChatGPT, I created compelling marketing materials and engaging online content that attracted a wider audience, boosting my business's online presence and reach.

The discovery of ChatGPT was serendipitous, yet it marked a turning point in my career. Initially sceptical, I quickly realised this tool's immense potential for enhancing business practices. It has empowered me to write and communicate with newfound confidence, liberating me from the fear of spelling or grammar mistakes. The AI's ability to understand and respond to a wide variety of topics made it an ideal partner in my writing endeavours, allowing me to focus on the creative aspects of my work without the constant worry of dyslexia-related mistakes.

In fact, the impact of ChatGPT on my business has been so profound that I decided to set myself a challenge – to write and publish a book in just four weeks, using ChatGPT for all aspects of the writing process. Not only did I meet this ambitious goal, but the book, 'The Accidental Legacy: Empowering Coaches to Leave a Profound Imprint,' became a testament to the capabilities of this

AI tool. This book, created entirely using ChatGPT, covered various topics, from creating high-quality content to crafting engaging social media posts and powerful sales copy.

ChatGPT has become an indispensable tool in my business in just a short time. It has allowed me to focus on what really matters – creating value for my clients and customers – while streamlining my writing process and improving my communication and marketing quality. The possibilities with ChatGPT seem endless, from generating ideas to creating engaging content that resonates with audiences.

As I continue to use ChatGPT in my business, I am excited to see what new opportunities and challenges it will present. I am confident that with the help of this fantastic tool, I will be able to achieve my goals and continue to make a positive impact in the world. ChatGPT has transformed my approach to writing and communication and enabled me to empower other coaches and entrepreneurs to embrace this technology and unlock its full potential in their businesses.

Not only has ChatGPT been instrumental in helping me find my voice, but it has also had a similar impact on my clients. They, too, can now express themselves in ways they weren't before, whether through the written word or by creating AI digital art. The gift of ChatGPT has opened the door to limitless opportunities, making what once seemed impossible possible. Its versatility and accessibility have enabled my clients and I to explore and express our creativity in new, exciting ways.

The influence of ChatGPT extends beyond just personal development; it has also catalysed the creation of new services in my business. This is a testament to the comprehensive training and underlining methodology I've developed, incorporating ChatGPT's capabilities. For instance, I've been able to design unique coaching programs that leverage AI for more personalised and effective client engagement. These programs utilise ChatGPT's ability to generate tailored responses and scenarios, enhancing the coaching experience.

Moreover, the integration of ChatGPT has allowed me to offer innovative services like AI-assisted content creation and digital art workshops. These services diversify my business offerings and provide clients with novel ways to explore their creativity and personal growth. They have become popular among my clientele, further solidifying my business's position as a forward-thinking, tech-savvy coaching service.

The transformation of my business practices with ChatGPT is not just about technological advancement; it's about redefining what's possible in the coaching industry. It has enabled me to break traditional boundaries and offer services that truly stand out. This evolution has been fulfilling on a professional level and immensely rewarding as I witness its profound impact on my clients.

As I look to the future, the possibilities with ChatGPT continue to excite and inspire me. This tool has revolutionised my business and played a pivotal role in shaping the future of coaching and personal development. By embracing ChatGPT and other cutting-edge technologies, my coaching practice will continue to grow and significantly impact my clients' lives.

In conclusion, ChatGPT has been a game-changer in both my personal journey with dyslexia and in the trajectory of my coaching business. Its impact on communication, creativity, and business growth is undeniable. As I continue exploring and integrating this technology, I am excited about its endless opportunities for innovation and success.

"Embracing ChatGPT has been like unlocking a door to a new world where the limitations of dyslexia no longer define my capabilities. This gift has not only transformed my approach to communication and creativity but has also redefined the boundaries of what's possible in my coaching business. It's a testament to the power of technology in turning what once seemed impossible into a realm of new, exciting opportunities for both me and my clients."

Unlocking Insights: Empowering Coaches and Therapists for Transformation

I've gained valuable insights that can apply to anyone facing challenges in their personal or professional journey. Here are the top five key takeaways:

1. Resilience in the Face of Adversity: My journey truly highlights the power of resilience. Despite facing early struggles and formidable challenges, I found the inner strength to persevere, adapt, and keep moving forward. This resilience has become an invaluable quality that has not only

helped me overcome obstacles but can also serve as a guiding light for individuals navigating their own challenges in various aspects of life.

2. Self-Empowerment: My story deeply underscores the significance of self-empowerment. I refused to let dyslexia define my limitations or hinder my pursuit of my dreams. Instead, I consciously embraced technology and my unique life journey, ultimately seizing control of my professional destiny. This profound sense of empowerment has the potential to inspire others to take charge of their own lives, break free from limitations, and achieve their aspirations.

3. Embracing Technology: The seamless integration of ChatGPT into my life and business vividly demonstrates the transformative power of technology. By harnessing the capabilities of AI tools, I not only conquered the challenges associated with dyslexia but utilised technology to elevate my communication, amplify my creativity, and propel my overall business success. This serves as a powerful testament to the pivotal role that technology can play in overcoming personal and professional obstacles.

4. Innovation in Coaching: My innovative coaching approach, which seamlessly incorporates ChatGPT's capabilities, illuminates the importance of remaining open to new methods and cutting-edge technologies in the coaching industry. Through this approach, I have offered distinctive services that provide a highly personalised experience for clients, extending the reach of my business and making a substantial impact on those I work with. This pioneering spirit showcases the potential for transformative change when embracing innovative tools.

5. Continuous Growth and Learning: My unwavering commitment to personal development and ongoing growth is a recurring theme throughout my journey. From conquering self-esteem issues to constantly exploring and integrating emerging technologies, I have demonstrated that the path of learning and growth is perpetual. This steadfast dedication to self-improvement is a valuable lesson for all individuals on their quest to achieve their goals, reminding them that self-discovery and enhancement are lifelong endeavours.

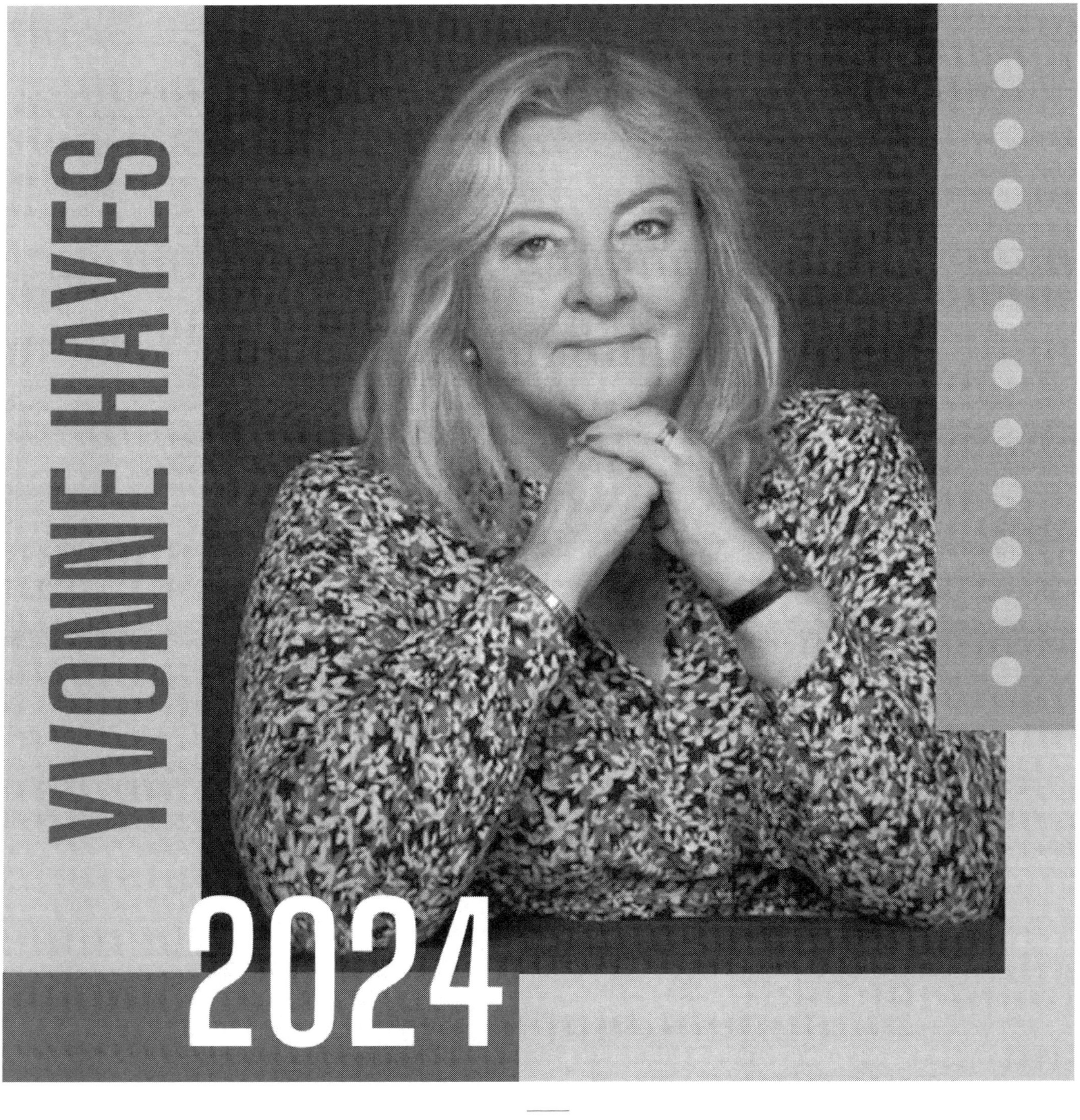
YVONNE HAYES
2024

CHAPTER 22

The 12th Cracker

By Yvonne Hayes

The scene was set, and we lined up at the front of the classroom – super excited to be chosen as the principal poem in the forthcoming Christmas Concert. This is as big as it gets for a 6-year-old in the top Infants class. We did not yet know what the poem was about, but out of a class of almost 40, being in the top 12 filled me with pride.

Miss Riches was a vision of the 1960s Miss Trunchball or 'The Governess' clad in her menacing grey suit and heavy brogues. Not a woman to question but to merely obey!.

The parts were given out – 12 verses, so one for each of us.

I was to be the final verse, so I felt anxious yet proud to have that part – **I** would be the one everyone would remember!

The Poem was about 12 crackers – all presented beautifully in an ornate box, each one bright and colourful with pretty bows and glitter, containing crinkly hats, mottos, jokes and a surprise toy – how exciting. In turn, each child recited their verse explaining what was inside – the motto, the hat, the toy and the snap. There had been no time to look at our parts beforehand as we had taken ages to tidy up after art! Here goes …

Pop! The first child went – Simon – a timid boy with a little voice – and a very underwhelming pop. But his toy was a magnificent toy sports car - the excitement of playing with that and travelling to imaginary destinations.

Bang! The second child went – Judith, my best friend. She had a huge bellowing voice, and it certainly woke everyone up! Her toy was a bouncing ball, which she took great joy in actually bouncing – which quickly disappeared over the desks, resulting in a glowering glare – the 'Miss Riches **LOOK**'.

Crack! Off went the 3rd child – Peter – Miss Riche's favourite – the angel-faced boy who could do no wrong – of course, he had a pack of coloured pencils – such visions and dreams could be drawn with those.

On it went with various noises which set us giggling as each 'pop' was rendered with varying degrees of loudness and hilarity.

Then my turn came … I was ready … I had planned my 'pop' in my head – not too loud, not too quiet, just exciting enough to raise a head and I was intrigued to see what my gift would be.

Silence … no pop … my cracker was pulled to a deathly hush …. I guess there was still a hat, a toy and a motto, even a funny joke … but I was too upset to notice – after all, what was the point of a cracker with no pop?

I remember nothing more of that day – whether or not we performed in the Christmas concert – all I could think about was that I had no 'pop'.

Why me? What had I done to upset the mighty Miss R? Was I being punished for being too chatty, for being too quiet, for being me? I was not going to share the experience with my mum and dad after all – nothing to be proud of – whoever heard of a cracker with no pop.

Over the next few weeks, the harrowing experience popped back into my head, but eventually, I pushed it to the back of my mind and got on with life.

Over the years, I have performed successfully and obtained O-levels, A-levels, a Bachelor's Degree, several Postgraduate courses and a Master's Degree, which leads others to believe I am capable, competent and intelligent.

However, despite having several opportunities over the past 55 years, I have always taken the safest route, the least scary job, the opportunity that doesn't push me out of my comfort zone, as, after all – I am just ordinary, a failure almost who has just been fortunate in obtaining the roles I have had, as I am still the cracker with no 'pop'.

I have always believed that I am average, nothing spectacular – I may look like everyone else, but I have no spark inside. Even my resting face is boring and grumpy! My clothes are safe and keep me in the background, although I secretly want to **POP!**

Until… I met a lady who miraculously opened me up and gently pulled this story out of my subconscious, revealing my fear of 'popping'.

This story had never been told until that day – I had held it safely inside for 55 years – not daring to let it out.

The release was overwhelming – I have always wanted to 'pop' - to be noticed, to be special - to be a 'cracker' of a person.

The encounter with this Mentor and the final release of this life-limiting memory was empowering. I had focused for 55 years on the one thing that was 'wrong' with the cracker – it had no snap. I had totally failed to see that it was still beautiful on the outside, bright and glittery with beautiful ribbons; it still had a motto to live by, a joke to lift people's souls, and a toy to bring joy. What was on the inside was amazing and of value, and who needs to be noisy to be noticed anyway? We can all be quietly beautiful (both inside and out), bringing joy to ourselves and others.

The reframing of this story has been empowering - resulting in a growth of self-belief. I have experienced a total mindset shift. I can now focus on my many strengths - BELIEVE in myself and my unfolding, exciting future.

This can be true for all of us – what is your limiting belief?

What is holding you back?

Believe you can achieve anything you want to – we can all POP in our own way and stand out.

BELIEVE YOU CAN ACHIEVE

When working in Business, especially in these ever-changing times, working alone or in isolation can often be tough, and we can

- **Doubt our potential…so…**
- **Our confidence dips…and…**
- **We feel dis-empowered**

It is time to Boost your self-belief. It is time to realise how much potential you have.

When we doubt our potential, we let Limiting Beliefs in, and we question whether we have the ability, the product or the service needed for success.

"Our responsibility is to rise from mediocrity to competence, from failure to achievement. Our task is to become our best selves." [Thomas S. Monson, 1987]

Ask yourself these questions …

- Who else has achieved the goals you seek?

- What positive beliefs do they hold? Use these as Mentors! Surround yourself with positive people

- What difficult things have you succeeded in doing in the past? Winners use the past as a great resource

- What strengths do you have? Write these down; praise and positive self-talk are key to self-empowerment.

It is time to grow in confidence. Extract the learning in each situation. "I don't fail at anything; I successfully find ways that don't work" [Thomas Edison]

"Courage is not the absence of fear, but a triumph over it" [Nelson Mandela].

Appreciate your inner wisdom. "It's not about the resources, it's about the resourcefulness" [Warren Buffet]

Have a Winner's Mindset

Make decisions & rarely change your mind

Always aim for the top & the end target

Use mental rehearsal to 'feel' like a winner

Take massive, bold action

Write down your new empowering belief

It's time to become Self-Empowered

Winners leave their comfort zone and do whatever it takes. The most influential person in any group is the one who is the most flexible – that is certainly true of those businesses that are surviving and thriving post-lockdown.

Winners know the value of time and use it wisely – have we planned our 2-5 year goals, broken them down into annual, quarterly, monthly and weekly goals (or even daily tasks)?

"Be the change you wish to see in the world" [Gandhi]

I have 'sacked' the boss, left the 'safe' day job behind and am now continuing my journey of self-discovery and working out my own path in life, doing what I love best – FAMILIES, FOCUS & FOREVER .... But that is another story.

Discover what makes you POP and what makes your heart sing?

Epilogue

We hope you enjoyed reading this book and have taken a lot from the lessons these ladies are sharing.

If you would like to be in the next book, get in touch with **sharon@thebookchief.com**

Everyone has a story to share and everyone can benefit from reading someone's story. Would you like someone to benefit from reading yours?

Get to know the Authors!

CHAPTER 1 – MRS FRECKLES

Just a girl with a passion for creativity, a love of writing, and a message for anyone else that may be struggling that there is hope and there is a way forward!

CHAPTER 2 – GILLIAN ROUTLEDGE

Gillian is an author and guide on the transformative journey of 'Discovering the Love Within.' She is the founder of The Awaken to Love approach. Her personal story serves as a testament to her commitment to helping others reconnect with love in its purest form. With honesty and vulnerability, Gillian shares from her own trials in life, offering solace and relatability to those facing similar challenges. Through her book, Gillian unravels life changing tools and insights aimed at healing old wounds and revitalising fractured relationships. Gillian offers talks and programs tailored for individuals, couples and groups.

Business Details:

Soul Journey | **www.gillianroutledge.com**

CHAPTER 3 – HEATHER WILDMAN

Heather is a Cumbrian lass from the Lake District. Brought up on a family beef and sheep hill farm in the small valley of Lorton located between Keswick and Cockermouth. Heather has always lived and been involved in agriculture and in her own words, was very lucky as a child to be brought up on a farm where she could make camps in the hay barn, help lamb the sheep and feed and play with the orphan lambs and calves.

An idyllic lifestyle, Heather never lost her love for farming and the countryside. She now resides in the South West of Scotland and is the mother to two gorgeous girls, Charlotte 22 and Nicola 21. She is divorced and living with her partner Fergus on a large 1200 cow dairy farm which looks onto the stunning Cumbrian fells.

Heather is a business owner and runs Saviour Associates Ltd which allows her to work in the field she loves so much, agriculture.

Business Details:

Saviour Associates Ltd | www.saviourassociates.co.uk | info@saviourassociates.co.uk

CHAPTER 4 – JO HOWARTH

Jo Howarth is an advanced hypnotherapist and mindfulness practitioner. She runs The Happiness Club and teaches people how to look after their mental health and emotional wellbeing. She has two beautiful daughters, two gorgeous cats and one very naughty dog.

The Happiness Club is a monthly membership club where members receive daily support from, and 24/7 access to, qualified therapists. Jo also works with corporate organisations that are committed to supporting their employees. She works within schools to teach students techniques to develop their resilience. There is also a team of Happiness Club Trainers that deliver resilience training to corporates and our programmes to schools across the world.

Jo is an inspirational speaker and bestselling author of six books. In 2017, she won two national awards for her work in The Happiness Club. In 2020, she was the Runner Up for North West Entrepreneur of the Year, the only female finalist.

Jo also trains people to become CPD-accredited Happiness Club Trainers, delivering our business and school programmes across the UK, New Zealand and Canada. She trains people to become qualified, GHR-accredited, advanced hypnotherapists.

Business Details:

The Happiness Club | www.thehappinessclub.co.uk | jo@thehappinessclub.co.uk

CHAPTER 5 – JULIA JONES

Hi Im Julia, I became an entrepreneur three years ago. I work in the corporate learning space, specialising in soft skills and self-awareness development. While I am lucky enough to work with clients across the globe, I much prefer it when clients visit our classroom; six acres of pasture in Staffordshire where my herd of horses reside (aka the Subject Matter Experts!).

Previously I was Head of Global Training & Education for a psychometric test publisher. I worked there for 17 years.

I am a mum of three amazing dustbin-lids and you could say I've lived life so far, the hard way!

Business Details:

Altezza People UK Ltd | www.altezzapeople.co.uk | julia@altezzapeople.co.uk

CHAPTER 6 – KERRY TUSCHOFF

Founder and Director of Hypnobabies Hypnobirthing Childbirth Education, Kerry Tuschhoff has loved being a childbirth educator, doula, speaker, and hypnotherapist for over 30 years. Teaching families to trust in their minds, bodies, babies, and the process of childbirth is her passion, and hearing healing birth stories is her joy! Educating people who need change and healing, about the life-altering benefits of therapeutic hypnosis for many physical, emotional, and financial issues is also paramount to Kerry.

Business Details:

Hypnobabies Hypnobirthing | www.hypnobabies.com | director@hypnobabies.com

CHAPTER 7 – KEZZABELLE AMBLER

11th Bard of Northampton, Pushcart Prize nominee, speaker and published performance poet Kezzabelle Ambler playfully weaves her wit, wisdom and humour into her one-woman spoken word show 'Permission To Love Yourself' connecting through her Forget-Me-Not Days bespoke retreats, 'Weaving Words' creative writing workshops to express, heal and play with words, which gives people 'Permission To Speak' (the title of her fifth book and audio) She tours the country baring all in her craft, blessing and encouraging whoever crosses her path, giving a voice to their story, their pen becomes a tool for life.

Business Details:

Weaving Words | www.kezzabelle.co.uk | QR Code is for Audio Poem, 'REFUGE'

CHAPTER 8 – LENORA SCURRY

Lenora is an Author, Life Coach, and Motivational Speaker who uses the wisdom of her own experiences to help women achieve better relationships with self and others at a more conscious level. She believes the practice of self-love and setting healthy boundaries allows women to become more empowered to reach their full potential by living a life of purpose, ON purpose.

Lenora was an Advertising and Marketing professional with thirty-five years of experience. She has earned many certificates for her outstanding sales record and most importantly her dynamic customer service skills.

She volunteers for numerous women's shelters proving her expertise, including Teen Challenge where she worked closely with the residents and their children to bring hope and light to their circumstances.

As the previuos Owner of Skyline Consulting, an advertising company, she applies her ability to closely connect with people and create success for them with her outstanding media expertise and customer service.

Business Details:

www.lenorascurry.com

CHAPTER 9 – LISA POGSON

Lisa is the Managing Director of Airmaster, the heating and cooling specialists, and has grown into a £10 million turnover Mechanical Services Contractor. She has been a member of Women in Refrigeration Air Conditioning and Heat Pumps Committee for the last 3 years. Lisa was part of the first national cohort of the Goldmab Sachs 10,000 small businesses programme. She is an active member of the business community as a STEM Ambassador, a Freeman of the Company of Cutlers of Hallamshire and for 3 years she was the first female president of the combined Barnsley and Rotherham Chamber of Commerce.

Business Details:

Airmaster Air Conditioning Ltd | www.airmaster.uk.com | team@airmaster.uk.com

CHAPTER 10 – MARIE-LOUISE O'NEILL

Marie-Louise specialises in branding and Canva design, offering a range of logo and design services, training and is an official Canva Creator. Bringing together 20 years in the design industry, a branding degree and sprinkle in Canva for a winning combination.

She loves to work with entrepreneurs, coaches, marketing experts and virtual assistants to create consistent content that's on brand but with the flexibility to evolve over time. Power up your designs with her help using her free app 'Build a brand with Canva'.

Business Details:

Lovely Evolution | www.lovelyevolution.co.uk | ml@lovelyevolution.co.uk

CHAPTER 11 – MARLENE NEUMANN

Marlene gently takes people on a spiritual journey of deep understanding towards themselves through the power of nature and photography. She guides those that are curious and seeking a new path. For the past 40 years, based on her own life experiences, she has been teaching people to reawaken what they were instinctively born knowing.

She knows the importance of appreciating every single moment of existence, in nature, and she wholeheartedly teaches others to do the same.

Marlene is an exceptional woman living her life on purpose in service to the earth and all of its inhabitants.

Business Details:

The Voice of Nature | www.thevoiceofnature.net | hello@thevoiceofnature.net

CHAPTER 12 – NAOMI RICHES MBE PLY DL

I spent a decade as an elite athlete in the GB Rowing Team. Years of dedication working in a high-pressured performance environment, adapting to a huge variety of people and pushing my mind and body to its limits… but it was worth it with a Gold at the London 2012 Paralympic Games, a Bronze in Beijing 2008 and six World Titles.

My passion is helping others to maximise their strengths and minimise the sabotage; allowing them to perform at their peak. I do this through motivational speaking, group facilitation, one to one and group coaching.

Business Details:

www.naomiriches.com | info@naomiriches.com

CHAPTER 13 – REBECCA LEEK SMITH

Hi! I'm Rebecca, an artist, group facilitator, inspirational speaker and textiles designer based in Stafford uk. That's the professional bit, but also a mother, charity shop addict, and survivor of domestic abuse. Growing up with domestic abuse and spending my younger years in predomina tely domestic abuse relationships, I was a bit late to the party graduating at 45 years old, but I fin ally did it, with a first in textiles and surface pattern and winning 2 awards (little happy dance)! M y mission is now creating art works, supporting victims and survivors, and raising awareness of domestic abuse.

Business Details:

Instagram: www.instagram.com/becky20_art

CHAPTER 14 – REBECCA RYAN

Rebecca Ryan is a teacher and a multi-award winnjng singer from Northamptonshire. She is more at home writing songs as part of her musical duo Tu-kay & Ryan, but was excited to embrace the challenge of writing a piece for Successful Women.

Business Details:

www.Tukayandryan.co.uk

CHAPTER 15 – RITA PRESTON

Rita Preston left the income tax profession at the end of 2021 (after 32 years) to pursue writing on a full-time basis, collaborating in several volumes to date.

She received the 2021 Golden Quill Award from A.B.A.T.E. of Pennsylvania and is honored to be an Ambassador for Mo2vate Magazine, Rita's writing is blossoming just as she dreamt of as a child in primary school. Her first solo book, My Life is a Meme, is in the works. She loves motorcycling with her husband, savors time with grandchildren, and is involved in several community organizations.

Business Details:

www.ritaprestonsviews.com | rita@ritaprestonsviews.com

CHAPTER 16 – SARA NYSTROM

Sara Nystrom, the visionary leader behind Communication Queen, drives global change by enhancing women's communicative impact. Co-founder of the World Women Organization, she's acclaimed as "Most Inspiring Woman of the Year" and "Women's Empowerer of the Year." A seasoned polyglot, Sara's cross-cultural commitment spans 70+ countries, and she speaks 8 languages. Rooted in Africa with a Master's in African Studies, Sara's Nigerian experiences earned her the cherished name 'Omobowale'—'The child returned home.' Recognised with the Chieftaincy title of Oju-Oge, she is greatly esteemed in the Ilado-Ikoko Kingdom. A licensed Mind Trainer, certified Body Language Master Trainer, and Impact Coach, Sara empowers individuals and organisations, including impactful work at the United Nations office in Geneva.

Business Details:

Communication Queen AB | www.beacommunicationqueen.com

info@beacommunicationqueen.com

CHAPTER 17 – SUE BLACKWELL

I believe in a society where everyone belongs as equals including those historically marginalised. I witness innovative thinking creating equal opportunities for all. We all need the right support to tap into our unique potential and allow our own voice to be heard in the language that is right for us. Challenging the status quo comes naturally. Changing systems takes a little longer but by harnessing the power of co-production, love and respect everyone is empowered to be the best that they can be; a contributor to life. I share, encourage and inspire others through talks, workshops and my writing.

Business Details:

www.blackwells.biz | sue@blackwells.biz

CHAPTER 18 – SUE POWELL

My name is Sue Powell, I am a children's author/nursery nurse and work in the NHS with 0-5 years and families. I use my 45 years' experience of working with children when writing my books and love doing readings, answering questions, and nurturing the love of books in them. In my spare time I enjoy lots of arts and craft activities dabbling in cake decorating, silver smithing, stained glass, pottery, gardening and reading. I have a quirky, off beat sense of humour, am very clumsy and once fell in the canal when visiting my mother-in-law who lives on a narrowboat.

Business Details:

SMBBook@virginmedia.com

CHAPTER 19 – TRACEY-JANE HUGHES

Tracey-Jane inspires people to listen courageously and create lasting transformational change in every part of their life.

Through her own journey she has learnt that creating the space to listen is key to personal, career and business success. Her loving and compassionate approach allows space for others to listen to themselves.

Tracey-Jane supports people to explore, have fun and be curious on their adventure through life. She believes in the power of connection and learning with and from nature.

Through mentoring and coaching she empowers people to have the courage to listen to take the next step in their life.

Business Details:

www.tracey-jane.com | t-j@tracey-jane.com

CHAPTER 20 – WAIRIMU WAROBI

Born in Hackney, London, Wairimu returned to England in 2001 for an adventure. Her career spans corporate and international NGOs in Kenya. She worked for 17 years in Social Care and the NHS in England and has lived in Zimbabwe, South Africa, and Ghana.

Wairimu is a mental health activist and ambassador for a non-profit UK organisation, The Nous, who create awareness for Black Asian and ethnic minorities. Being a trade union representative gave her a platform to represent members, particularly disabled members. As a Manager, she supported her staff in promotions and transforming career goals. She shares information on different global platforms.

Wairimu received the Little Effects Award for empowering women in 2017. She also co-authored "Singled Out", which highlights the epidemic of bullying and harassment in the workplace, and she is an Author in her own right, having a Best-Selling book called 'Wounded: Diary of a Nameless Woman.

Wairimu also writes as a contributor for The Mighty.com, a non-profit USA organisation and has been a contributing writer for MO2VATE Media, gaining the Editors Choice Acknowledgement in June 2020.

She is currently rebuilding her life after leaving her career following a diagnosis of fibromyalgia and lupus and the effects of long-term COVID. She continues to write.

Business Details:

Afrobrit Ramblings (Podcast) | www.anchor-fm/lady-boss

CHAPTER 21 – WENDY KIER

As a visionary founder, dedicated coach, and tireless advocate for women, Wendy Kier is the epitome of a multi-dimensional leader. Her expertise spans a broad spectrum—from personalised coaching and mentoring to cutting-edge AI technology—reflecting her commitment to having a transformative impact on both her clients and the coaching industry at large.

In a world longing for change, Wendy Kier emerges as a true catalyst. She is not merely committed to doing business but is invested in enriching the world, one coaching programme at a time. When you engage with Wendy, you're not just receiving a service; you're becoming a part of a vision—a vision that is as informative as it is inspirational.

Business Details:

www.wendykier.com | wendy@wendykier.com

CHAPTER 22 – YVONNE HAYES

I am a Parenting & Lifestyle Coach & Goal Mapping Consultant. I deliver 1-2-1 and group support to help people nurture themselves, build family unity, beat stress and achieve their potential.

I am an International Business Owner promoting health and wellbeing. Within this I act as a Business Mentor for my Team.

I have 20 years' experience as a Psychology lecturer and 15 years' experience as an accredited Parenting facilitator. I am a qualified in Reflexology, Indian Head Massage and Neuro-Linguistic Programming (NLP).

I find all of these different skills and experiences help me to stay calm and stress-free in a very busy life.

Business Details:

www.yvonne-hayes.com | hello@yvonne-hayes.com

About the Creator / Publisher of this Book

SHARON BROWN owns the Multi-Award Winning 'The Book Chief Publishing House', gaining 'Book Publisher of the Year 2023' and again in 2024 by the Innovation & Excellence Awards. Sharon has always loved helping small business owners achieve the credibility they deserve and through The Book Chief and its associated businesses, she has created an experience that helps Authors and Business Owners really build their personal and business brands. This includes a media platform and public speaking business.

Sharon moved to the West Midlands in 2003 from Glasgow, Scotland, and has a wide-ranging career in Event Management, Marketing, Project Management and board-level support in various industries.

In 2006, as a side line, Sharon started the first Speed-dating business in the West Midlands at the height of its popularity, which ran for two consecutive successful years.

In 2015, Sharon started her own Corporate Events Agency but quickly realised that business was heading online, so she created and launched a platform that she had been looking for but couldn't find elsewhere. Revival Sanctuary was born in 2018 to create an environment of 'Collaboration over Competition'. Sharon still has a group with many original members, but she retired from the Commercial side of this platform last year to concentrate on her passion… writing and publishing!

Two further projects were launched during lockdown (2020) to help small business owners build their brands through speaking, writing, publishing, and collaborative working. MO2VATE Magazine was created in six weeks from concept to implementation and received a fantastic following from its subscribers and supporters. It's now had a complete facelift as MO2VATE Media, evolving as a membership-driven business and information hub where business owners can upload articles and press releases to share their news and knowledge.

The Speakers Index was the third platform to be launched as Sharon saw a gap in the market around Speaking Agencies and the need for more promotion towards their speakers. The Speakers Index is relaunching as an 'all-round' speakers' platform in late Spring 2024, with four new partners coming on board to reshape it into something spectacular.

The Book Chief Publishing House was Sharon's latest project, launched in 2021 with an impressive portfolio of clients and Authors. Over 250 Authors from 15 countries worldwide have been published through The Book Chief.

Sharon's vision was to provide an affordable publishing service, turning small business owners into credible authors through a robust and structured process. The Book Chief portfolio has exponentially grown during 2022 and 2023, welcoming Authors from around the world with some notable high profile clients to date. It continues to build huge momentum, onboarding clients mainly through referral marketing and retained Author portfolios. The Book Chief has recently added Audio Books to their list of services too amongst a wealth of other book enhancing services, creating a one-stop-shop for Authors of all genres.

Services

The Book Chief Publishing House

The Book Chief Publishing House was born during the latter end of the pandemic with a mission to support business owners and lovers of writing, on their path to becoming credible Authors.

The Book Chief publishes every age group, genre, type and size of book and advises on every step of producing Authors books from book covers, titles, book descriptions, and growing through the relevant rankings on Amazon and much more.

The Book Chief has a great track record in customer service and of producing great results for Authors books, in layout, editing, design and marketing.

As a one-stop shop for all Publishing needs, and payment plans to spread the cost, it should be the first stop for those looking to publish and spread the word about their book! Lots of additional services to choose from too!

www.Thebookchief.com

sharon@thebookchief.com

MO2VATE Media (formerly MO2VATE Magazine)

MO2VATE Media is a global digital business hub covering topics across business industries, health, inspiration, lifestyle, politics, opinion / research-based information, entrepreneur insights and many other topics, founded by Sharon Brown.

All articles are written by business owners and the project is managed by independent entrepreneurs. The online hub runs yearly International Awards and produces various books written by the Contributors who are part of the MO2VATE community.

www.Mo2vatemedia.com

editor@mo2vatemagazine.com

The Speakers Index

The Speakers Index is an online directory for speakers and event organisers designed to improve their chances of being seen by the right people.

We produce a quarterly magazine where each speaker features on a double page spread. The magazine is sent out through social media and to our email list on each publication.

Working similar to an agency but without any additional fees or commission, The Speakers Index also creates events to allow speakers to participate and be seen.

www.Thespeakersindex.com

sharon@thespeakersindex.com

Printed in Great Britain
by Amazon

38674629R00112